THIRD YEAR SURVIVAL GUIDE

CONNOR WHITELEY

No part of this book may be reproduced in any form or by any electronic or mechanical means. Including information storage, and retrieval systems, without written permission from the author except for the use of brief quotations in a book review.

This book is NOT legal, professional, medical, financial or any type of official advice.

Any questions about the book, rights licensing, or to contact the author, please email connorwhiteley@connorwhiteley.net

Copyright © 2024 CONNOR WHITELEY

All rights reserved.

DEDICATION
Thank you to all my readers without you I couldn't do what I love.

INTRODUCTION

A lot of students say that your final year at university is the scariest, most stressful and most intimidating year of your undergraduate degree. There might be some truth in that but I'm here to show you that your Final year can be a lot of fun, mostly stress-free and it can be the best year of your undergraduate degree.

I really mean it.

If you want to learn more about dissertations (or Final Year Projects as they are sometimes called), what to do after your undergrad, how your exams work and more. Then this is a brilliant guide and book that is packed filled with useful and easy-to-understand tips about how to make the most of your third and final year at university.

What Will This Book Cover?

To help you overcome any worries, stressors and concerns you have about your final year, I want to cover as much as possible and I wanted to include topics that I wished I knew before I started my final year.

Therefore, the book can be broken down into four sections:

- Introduction To Your Final Year- this covers topics like the importance of a positive mindset, essay writing tips, experience with optional modules and more to help you before your final year starts.
- Final Year Project- this covers all my tips and tricks about the dissertation. Including data collection, why this is fun and many more useful topics that I really wished I had known before I started.
- What to do after university- covers all the different options you could do including what my friends and myself are doing after our undergraduates.
- Exams- this covers important topics like revision, the relief you feel afterwards, how the exams work and more.

All before wrapping up with my hopeful, inspiring and positive final chapter on my favourite moments from my final year and why this has been my favourite year of my university journey.

Why Buy This Book?

Just like all of my other books, this is a fun brilliant fact-based book that is delivered in an engaging, conversational tone that actually brings the subject material alive. This is NOT a boring, dull book at all and it is packed filled with useful experiences based on my own final year so you can get first-hand experience about these topics.

Therefore, if you want an excellent guide to your Final Year at university delivered in an easy-to-understand and engaging tone that won't make you want to fall asleep then this is definitely the book for you.

Bonus

As there is an entire section of this book talking about Final Year Projects and dissertations, I have included my own one at the back of the book without graphs, data outputs and references so you can see how a good one is written in case you find that useful.

Who Am I?

Personally, I always love to know who the author is of the nonfiction I read so I know the information is coming from a good source. In case you're like me, I'm Connor Whiteley, the internationally bestselling author of over 40 psychology books.

In addition, I am the host of *The Psychology World Podcast,* a weekly show exploring a new psychology topic each week and delivering the latest psychology news. Available on all major podcast apps and YouTube.

Finally, I am a psychology graduate studying a Clinical Psychology Masters at the University of Kent, England.

So now we know more about each other, let's dive into the great topic of your final year at university.

PART ONE: BEFORE YOUR THIRD YEAR AND BEYOND

THIRD YEAR SURVIVAL GUIDE

IMPORTANCE OF A POSITIVE MINDSET, WANTING TO MAKE THE MOST OF THIS YEAR AND AN OVERVIEW OF MY FINAL YEAR

You're in your final year of university, or maybe you bought this book because you're approaching your final year of university in September, congratulations either way. You are so close now to your graduation and finally getting your degree.

Now I decided to kickstart this book with this chapter because I wanted to introduce my own Final Year experience briefly and what led up to it so you can understand where I'm writing from. I think my experience will be a lot more relatable than you imagine, and I want to stress the importance of a positive mindset and why making the most of this year is so important.

Making The Most Of This Year

I know when I was starting my Final Year, I was nervous because everyone always makes this year sound so important, so critical and so awful if you make a mistake. I suppose there is some truth in that statement but honestly, your Final Year can be an amazing time at university if you simply allow yourself to enjoy it.

Since this is your Final Year at university. Afterwards you won't have any more undergraduate lectures, no more exams (probably) and most of your friends probably would move on to other universities or other pathways after you all finish your psychology degree.

In addition, after this year, you don't have access to academics, the resources and the online journals that everyone takes for granted during their undergraduate degrees.

That's why I firmly believe you really need to make the most of your Final Year because I'll definitely realise that I have technically "lost" a lot of things now that I'm not an undergraduate. Although, I don't mind this because I made sure I capitalised on all the opportunities I could as an undergrad in my final year.

My point here is that definitely don't have any regrets at the end of your year. If there's a society you've always wanted to join, do it. If there's ever been an opportunity in your department that you've wanted to do, do it. If there has ever been an academic you wanted to pick their brains, seriously do it.

Your Final Year is whatever you make it and

that's actually the entire point of this book. Sure, I'm going to give you a lot of unofficial tips, I'm going to explain how a Final Year in psychology works and I'm telling you how to have the most fun during this year.

But seriously, only you can make the most of this year and only you can empower yourself to take all the opportunities that come your way.

Seize the day as they say.

Why A Positive Mindset is Critical?

I think as psychology students we hear about this constantly, but never in terms of our final year but I believe that a positive mindset is even more important here compared to everyday life or even our past university years. Since your final year will be stressful as you research your project, write up your project, do all the other pieces of coursework and more.

There is a hell of a lot to do in your final year.

However, this isn't a bad thing, it isn't a scary thing, it isn't even worth concerning yourself about. All because it might be hard and stressful at times, but you need to look at all this work you're doing at university as something that will help you in the future.

It's going to help you get your degree, it's going to help you prepare for your masters or whatever else you decide to do after university and it's going to (hopefully) help you earn more money than people without a degree.

It's that positive mindset that will be useful over

time and on the bad days, which you will definitely have some, the positive mindset will help you to realise that everything will be okay and it is more than okay to struggle at times.

And definitely ask for help if you need to.

I firmly believe that me going into my Final Year with a positive mindset and me being determined to enjoy it helped me more than I can ever admit. It made me look out for and apply for opportunities, it got me excited at university and it helped me get joy from my Final Year.

And if you think I'm a nerdy, dedicated student, please note that I'm not. I'm seriously not, I'm very average but university is a lot of fun and you can go far with the right mindset and drive to succeed.

<u>An Overview Of My Final Year</u>

I wanted to put in this next section so you know where I stand as I am the person writing this, what my university life was like before my Final Year and how "bad" of a start I had to my Final Year. The entire point of this section is that if I can do great in my Final year then anyone can.

I say this because the problem with universities is that they don't teach you how to write academically and their learning resources are dire at times, so I really struggled with my academic writing and my coursework.

I wrote three essays during my first and second year at university for coursework. In order my scores were 58, 55 and 52 and in one of my second year online exams that required two essays, I got a 48.

So yes I was beyond dire and it wasn't like I wasn't trying either. I got one of my friends to sit me down who always got 78s and I studied his essay. That didn't help me. I looked at the university's resources. That seriously didn't help me. And by the end of my second year I was basically hopeless.

Thankfully, I did manage to still get onto my Placement Year (just think a year of work experience) with an academic at my university. And whilst I talk about that great experience in my book, Year In Psychology (I really recommend you read that too), the brief summary of that year that was my wonderful supervisor and his PhD student helped me with my academic writing immensely and they were brilliant.

I cannot thank them enough for what they did for me that year and how I helped them in return. They are the reason why I got a 68, 72 and 82 this year in my essays.

Moreover, because my placement supervisor was so excellent, kind and he did socials, I applied to do my Final Year project with him (it turned out he wanted me desperately too) so that's why I ended up working with him during my Final Year.

Overall, my entire point here is that a student can be struggling badly, and I mean beyond badly in my case but given the right support a student can do brilliantly and that can help them in their Final Year more than anyone could expect.

And that's why over the course of the book, I'll

be helping you, giving you tips and explaining my own experience so you know what to expect and how to thrive in your Final Year.

All whilst having a blast along the way.

EXPECTATION SETTING FOR FINAL YEAR MODULES

Personally, I think this is a brilliant second chapter to start off the book with because, whilst in a moment I'll actually do another chapter talking about my own up-to-date experiences of final year modules, this is a critical chapter so you understand to expect in your final year of university. And I definitely don't want you to experience the same annoyance and disappointment as I did when it came to this topic.

<u>Expectation Setting For Final Year Modules</u>

When it comes to your final year at university, lots of students have the option to choose some of their own modules. This allows you to customise your degree more towards your own interests, but as I write this, I have just finished choosing my modules and there were plenty of things I would have liked to know beforehand. Therefore, in this blog post, I'll talk about my own experience and give you some advice so you can hopefully avoid my "mistakes".

Why Should You Think About Your Modules Earlier?

Throughout your second year at university (or whatever the year before your final year is called), it's a great idea to look into what modules your university allows you to take next year. This means if there are plenty of choices for you, then it gives you a bit of extra time to decide the direction you want your final year to go in.

Additionally, thinking about it earlier allows you to weigh up what factors are important to you, and so you can find modules that meet those requirements. That bit can be slightly time consuming. For example, if you're better at coursework then you might want to choose modules that are more coursework focused.

How Does Choosing Your Final Year Modules Work: The Perception

Of course, everything in these blog posts are just my own opinions, thoughts and experiences. But I really don't see why any university would be different from these major points in this post.

Therefore, I fully believed when it came to choosing my optional modules for my final year. I would be given basically free rein to choose what I wanted because it was my degree and I wanted to learn about what I was interested in.

Also I thought I would be free to pick modules from almost any other school outside the School of Psychology.

Now I can almost feel some of you readers start

to sink a little as you might have realised where I'm going with this post. Some of you might have thought about doing a module you would never do normally, others might have wondered about trying a module in a different subject area in case you wanted to do a postgraduate degree in a completely different area to your bachelor's, and the rest of you might not have thought about this at all.

I don't blame you!

How Does Choosing Your Final Year Modules Work: The Reality

However, the reality is a lot more strict than I realised. Since I knew that I would have to follow my requirements set up by my psychology degree. I interpreted that as me having to do my four compulsory modules and I would have free rein on the last two.

Yet this was far from the case, because of two main reasons.

Firstly, I love copyright law and learning about the legal side of the entertainment industry. From copyright in regards to books to the entertainment law about Hollywood and other things. Mainly because an American friend of mine is doing a course in this at her university and whenever she spoke about it, I was really, really interested in the subject matter.

Therefore, when I discovered I was only able to choose certain modules within psychology, and very few outside of the school. I was a bit disappointed and that was why I wanted to do this post, so you understood that you cannot just choose your modules too freely.

Sorry if I've shocked some people. It's better that you know now about this and not get disappointed when it comes to choosing your modules.

Secondly... well that requires a tip-full section below.

<u>Make Sure You Read Your Requirement Like A Textbook For An Exam</u>

Granted that headline is a bit long for my liking but it is true. I have had to exchange a good amount (2) emails with the university staff in charge of sorting out final year modules, because of the requirements.

Since your modules will (might?) be divided into two groups. Group 1 as it was told to us was the more theoretical modules then Group 2 were the practical modules.

Personally I think that sounds really, really easy, because I have two optional modules left and my degree requires I choose one from each group. I should just do that shouldn't I?

Well no, because when it comes to registering interest in these modules for my final year online, there are no groups like that. Instead you have to pick from some slightly changed groups and then you're done.

<u>Tips:</u>

My biggest tip for you is to make sure you read your degree requirements when picking your modules. This you can easily find on your university website and you'll probably be emailed it again when it comes to choosing your modules.

However, I cannot stress enough just look at the groups within those requirements and you'll be fine. As well as I know not all of this makes perfect sense right now, but I promise you when it comes to choosing your modules. You will definitely be grateful for this little blog post and hopefully you'll remember some of this advice.

Personally, if I had read the degree requirements in the handbook instead of reading the other stuff the university emailed me. I definitely wouldn't have had this much trouble choosing my two optional modules. Since apparently I kept choosing modules that I was really interested in, but because the groups they were in weren't compatible with the degree requirements. I had to choose new ones.

Spare yourself that pain! Read your degree requirement in your course handbook!

What about one last tip?

In my opinion, I wouldn't really call this a tip but more of a common sense thing that gets overlooked. Just make sure the modules you pick don't give you more modules in one university term compared to the other.

For example, my compulsory modules were 2 in the Autumn term, 2 in the spring term. But because I was really interested in my first two optional modules, I didn't even think about checking what term they were in, so they were both in the spring term. Meaning I had 2 modules in the Autumn term, 4 in the Spring term.

Leading to some emails and that was why I had to choose new modules in the first place.

Therefore, make sure you check when your modules are in the university year and don't overload yourself, because you will have to change it.

Conclusion:

As always none of these blog posts are ever, ever meant to be negative. As well as the point of this post was just to get you to realise the reality of choosing modules, and making sure you avoid some of the minor pitfalls that I haven't.

And to be honest, choosing your final year modules is hardly a negative experience, it can actually be a lot of fun and get you excited for the next academic year and your future after that.

MY EXPERIENCE WITH FINAL YEAR MODULES

I actually wrote the blog post behind that last chapter before I had even started my Third Year and I definitely don't regret that because at the time, I was very disappointed, a little angry and not at all impressed with some of the options that I had chosen.

However, at the time of writing, I've now done my Third Year and I think it's useful for you to see how my optional modules turned out so you know that you might not get the modules you want, but you can still thrive.

Therefore, just to remind you, my optional modules were:

- Clinical Psychology 1
- Clinical Psychology 2
- Cognition In Action
- Mental Health (Second Year Module)

Now even though the two clinical psychology

modules weren't optional for me because I was doing the clinical psychology degree, they were optional for other people so that's my excuse.

Personally, I really love optional modules. They give you so much freedom to explore your passions, your interests and you can start to specialise early on so you can start to show interest in certain areas. Something that is always useful on applications to Masters programmes.

In terms of my two clinical psychology modules, I loved them, naturally. Clinical Psychology 1 was a little less interesting than Clinical 2, because it focused on the more theoretical stuff and the basics that I had already learnt through my own research, the podcast and in other places.

Yet Clinical Psychology 2 was simply brilliant. Since it focused a lot on Cognitive Behavioural Therapy for Eating Disorders, Anxiety, Depression and Psychosis. As well as it involved systemic work, trauma-informed practice and a whole bunch of other great topics.

I loved the module and it made me love clinical psychology even more.

That is certainly another benefit of choosing optional modules that you are passionate about, because you really enjoy them, you focus on them more and you can enjoy the lectures too.

Mental Health Comments

Personally, this was definitely a module that I was excited about because this was a module that was a Third Year one when I was still applying to the University of Kent. But because they always listen to their students, they moved it to the second year so those students could enjoy clinical modules too.

However, I was a little disappointed in it because there was a hell of a lot of overlap between Clinical 2 and Mental Health. Mainly because the same people were teaching it and I do completely understand why the university did this.

The amount of us taking both a Third Year and a Second year module was microscopic but it was a little disappointing.

However, the benefit of the module was that I got to watch and listen and enjoy my Final Year Project supervisor's lecture on the module twice. He is a brilliant lecturer so that was worth it.

And at the end of the day, the assessments were pieces of coursework that I aced (thankfully) so overall the module was great.

Cognition In Action Comments

Now if you cast your mind back to the last chapter, this was the module that I did not want to be taking. I seriously didn't. Cognition is not my interest and by God, did these lectures prove that beyond a shadow of a doubt.

I don't mind people searching how we see things, how gravity impacts our behaviour and how priming works (even though it doesn't). I just don't care enough about the research areas to want to learn anything about it.

Yet because I always endeavour to be a good student, I still did the coursework, wrote the Short Answer Questions (they were the most horrific things of my life) and the Seminar Report. I got a 2:1 in the module thankfully but I still hated it.

And the reason why I'm talking about this negative module is because, in university life, you will always encounter topics and modules that you just hate. Especially if you have been backed into a corner when silly university rules, and when this happens you do need to focus and *try* to enjoy the module.

I admit this will be next to impossible at times because some modules will be awful. Yet the entire point of being a university student is to learn, study and try to have fun along the way.

Sometimes you will certainly have to fake it before you make it, but if you manage to make a module slightly less unbearable then that is a win.

And come on, a module tends to be 12 weeks, you can survive 12 weeks with a positive mindset and a lot of willpower.

Overall, choosing your Final year modules at university doesn't have to be scary. It is a fun time where you can express your own interests, deepen your understanding of your favourite topics and just tailor your degree towards what *you* want it to be and not what everyone else wants your degree to be.

University might be short in the grand scheme of things, so definitely make sure you enjoy it as much as you can. Both outside the lecture theatre and within.

WHY CHOOSING A FINAL YEAR PROJECT WISELY IS CRITICAL?

Ask any university psychology student and they will tell you that the Final Year Project or dissertation, as it is called by some universities, is the most important part of your Final year at university. And as much as I want to say that it flat out isn't, I can't.

Your Final Year Project might not be as do-or-die as everyone makes out but it is critical and it will form a lot of your final grade for your Final Year.

Therefore, deciding on what Final Year Project you want to do is critical because your degree, your happiness and your ability to enjoy the next academic year basically depends on this single decision.

In addition, my Final Year Project was a cognitive psychology project (even though I hate cognitive psychology) studying transfer learning in retrieval-based learning tasks using EEG equipment so we could see the neuro-evidence involved in this type of learning for the first time.

How Do Students Go About Choosing A Final Year Project?

As a result in my experience, the way how choosing a Final Year Project works is that in May or June of your second year at university, you're emailed a list of projects that you can sign up for. This list includes all the projects that the psychology academics at your university are offering.

You can look at this list and find out the project title, description, name and how many people can apply for the topic.

This is where my first insider tip comes from. If you have a particular academic in mind that you want to work with, definitely email them before this list is published and they might hold a space for you until you can officially apply through the list.

As whenever a person signs up through this list, the student's information gets passed onto the academic so they can sort through the applications. This is why you normally have to email the academic as well so they can hear why you're interested in the project and want to work with them.

Yes, at times choosing a Final Year Project really is like a job application.

Anyway, after you've looked at this list, you need to decide what project you want to apply for. You might want to apply for a couple in case one of them gets oversubscribed but just follow your own university's advice about this part of the process.

However, when choosing your Final Year Project I cannot stress these factors enough when making your decision.

Why Is Choosing The Right Academic Important?

Every single year without fail I hear horror stories about students having a nightmare with their academic supervisor because of how busy and useless they are. The entire point of an academic supervisor is to help you, be there to answer questions and have meetings with you so you can do your best.

That all depends on the supervisor themselves.

This year I know a ton of students that were struggling with their Final Year Project because they couldn't get a meeting with their supervisor, their supervisor was rubbish at answering questions and students just had one problem after another with their supervisor.

How do you solve this?

Obviously by choosing a good supervisor, but if you're in your second year at university and you happen to run into some psychology third-years, definitely ask them about their supervisor and any horror stories they've heard.

You need this information so you can make an informed decision about what to do and who to pick as your supervisor.

Also, I want to mention that even the most boring-sounding project can be made brilliant by a great supervisor. For example, I have no interest at all in cognitive psychology and yet, I loved my Final Year Project because of the supervisor and his PhD student.

Your supervisor really can be the difference between a terrible Final Year Project and a great one. At least in terms of how much you enjoy it.

Finally, I should just say from what I've heard about supervisors from my friends this year. Avoid Heads of School because they always tend to be extremely busy and don't have time for Final Year Project students and the questions they want to ask.

Even though they would call me a liar, my friends would agree with me.

Why The Project Itself Is So Important?

I really doubt this would be a major surprise to you but choosing the right Final Year Project itself is so critical.

Let me just explain why in a very scary sentence. You will be spending the next academic year of your life researching this topic. Do you really want to be researching something you hate for the next year?

Of course not. You would hate that, your happiness would die and you would just hate your life.

I don't want that for you.

Therefore, you either need to choose a project that you naturally love, or you need to choose a project with a brilliant supervisor. That will make the next year so much better for you.

Personally, I decided on the latter because for my Final Year Project, I naturally would have loved a forensic or clinical psychology topic since these are the areas I love in psychology. Yet I don't like change, I wanted to be more social and I knew my supervisor from my placement year was brilliant and he did socials.

That's important for something I'll talk about later on.

Therefore, I decided to ado a Final Year Project with my placement supervisor because I knew how great he was, there would be socials and I knew I would have a lot of fun.

Also, I really wanted to experiment with EEG equipment so I choose that Final Year Project so I could use a certain type of equipment.

Overall, whenever it comes to choosing a Final Year Project, only you know what will make you happy, make you passionate and make you look forward to the year ahead. That is what a Final Year Project is all about.

You will be researching your Project for the next year and if you choose a project without thinking about it and what would make you happy then you might regret it. I've heard a lot of stories this year about students that have hated their Final Year Projects.

I don't want you to be one of them.

Therefore, please just think about your Final Year Project, consider what would make you happy and consider who you want your supervisor to be. All those factors are critical and might very well be the difference between a great Final Year and one that you hate.

3 ESSAY WRITING TIPS FOR FINAL YEAR PSYCHOLOGY STUDENTS

I really have to be honest with you, because I never ever thought I would be even remotely good enough to do this sort of chapter, where I'm able to give you some tips for academic writing so you can improve on your essays.

However, now I'm getting scores in the 60s, 70s and 80s, I am confident that I know what I'm doing when it comes to essays and critical reviews. Therefore, in this chapter, I'm going to be sharing three main tips to help you, and just like everything else in the book, none of this is official advice.

In addition, I do want to stress here that we need to talk about how to do academic writing more, because universities really do just assume that you know it. Of course, there will be university students that do know exactly how to write academically, there will be other students that just learn it naturally or through some method that I couldn't find. Then there will be students like me that just struggled no matter how hard they tried to learn it.

I'm doing this chapter for the students like me, because someone has to.

Real Academic Writing Doesn't Use The PEEL Structure

I'm not sure how internationally used this structure is, but in the United Kingdom, back in secondary school (High School) and even at university level from the university resources I found, we are taught to use the PEEL structure in our essays. Meaning that in each paragraph of the main body of the essay, we need to make a Point, show the evidence for it by talking about the study's aims, number of participants and more, explain the evidence and then link it back to the question.

Now in theory this sounds great because if you're arguing that persuasion is not influenced by genetic factors (completely random I know) then you make them as your point, you should show a study that supports your argument, explain what the study means for your point and then link it back to the essay question.

However, something that dawned on me during my placement year that all academic writing is the same, and all academic writing doesn't use the PEEL structure.

I don't really know how to describe real academic

writing but to be honest, the style and paragraphs of your essays should read like a literature review or something very similar. It is using studies to support your points that is important but you don't need to show what each study involved like the PEEL structure requires.

In addition, another reason why the PEEL structure is awful is because if you use one citation a paragraph then believe me, the snobby academics of the world will eat you alive by constantly banging on about how you haven't referenced it enough, provided enough evidence and you have showed no evidence of wider reading.

It is so annoying after a while.

Overall, my unofficial tip is to style your paragraphs after those found in a literature review.

<u>Criticising Theories</u>

I have to admit that this is something that is very new to me at the time of writing but it is a lot of fun if you open your mind to it. Since at a basic-level, we all know that every single psychology theory is "wrong" to the extent that they are all very, very reductionist and human behaviour is way too complex for these reductionist theories to be correct.

For example, to grossly oversimplify here, the behavioural approach to behaviour proposes that humans simply learn stuff and this stuff causes behaviours. That's great in some situations and it can explain sometimes, but then according to the behavioural approach then cognitive processes, thinking biases and more don't exist.

We know they do. That's why behaviourism and cognitive approaches tend to be combined because they do compliment each other rather well.

However, that is still very reductionist because cognitive and behavioural approaches to behaviour don't explain how social and biological factors impact human behaviour, family conflict and so many other areas of behaviour.

Therefore, in reality, we do need some kind of grand unifying theory of human behaviour but I know how complex and impossible that would be to create. Therefore, until someone way, way smarter than I am develops that and gets research for it then we have to criticise and point out the flaws in each theory in the hope of creating a better one.

As a result, in your essay, you can combat and bounce theories off each other using research support.

For instance, if you're writing about Cognitive Behavioural Therapy for Depression, you could write about how effective it is, but comment on how systemic and family factors still play a role in the condition and how CBT dismisses these research findings.

Sometimes in essays you need to look beyond the results of research and onto more of the theoretical stuff using research to backup your points.

I admit this is tricky but it can actually be fun, interesting and academics seem to like it.

Find Cool Stuff

If you've been a reader of mine for a whilst then you know, you really know that I never use the word *cool* in my writing, because I just don't like the word. Yet when it comes to academic writing and essays, there isn't really a better word, all because of two main reasons.

Firstly, if you find something really cool because your essay topic then this will show critical reading and critical thinking skills that goes beyond the lecture content, making you a lot more likely to get higher marks.

Secondly, whatever cool things you find will make you more interested in the topic so you can actually learn to enjoy your essays. Now I know that makes me sound like a nerd and I promise you I'm not and this is all true.

When I was writing by 3,000-word critical review on Cognitive Behavioural Theory for Depression because I was finding out a bunch of cool things about it that is never spoken about, I was actually enjoying the writing process. I definitely think that joy partly played a role in my high grade.

An example of some cool things I found when I was researching critical thinking points for an exam topic I later wrote about can be found here (an extract from my exam answer on Leadership):

However, whilst Transformational Leadership is an intervention to make leaders more effective and positive towards their employees, this concept is based on the base of stress is exclusively negative for employees. This essay argues a paradigm shift is needed because the current thinking of stress is exclusively negative does not meet current research findings. It is all in how a person perceives stress. For example, Jamieson et al. (2012) found participants who believed stress was an adaptive (positive) response to life events were healthier, happy and had stronger, more adaptive physiological responses towards negative life events. Therefore, this study suggests by reframing stress from negative to positive, this brings psychological and physiological benefits to the employees. Also, Keller et al. (2012) concluded people who believed stress negatively impacted them had poor mental and physical health including an increased risk of premature death, but the people in the study who believed stress helped them did not have any of these negative outcomes. This is further supported by Poulin et al. (2013) finding stress did not predict mortality rates in people who helped others, like friends and family members, but stress did predict mortality rates in people who did not demonstrate prosocial behaviour. All these studies demonstrate how reframing stress as a positive response to negative life events leads to a decrease in the negative mental and physical wellbeing this essay mentioned in the first two paragraphs. As a result, this essay recommends a paradigm shift away from the current negative thinking surrounding stress in the workplace so researchers can understand how stress *benefits* workers in the working environment instead of harming them.

Did you know that work-related stress can be good for you?

Overall, if you go out of your way to find cool things about your essay topic, not only are you more likely to get higher marks because of your evidence of critical reading and thinking. Yet your own enjoyment and motivation will increase too.

Which come on, during final year essays you seriously need that motivation.

MAKING FINAL YEAR FRIENDS AT UNIVERSITY

Whilst I am personally not sure how useful this chapter might be for psychology students, I still want to include it because this is very interesting, very personal and for certain people this will be a very important chapter that might help them for the rest of their lives.

Now I won't lie when I say that my university and life experience is unique in the sense that I basically had a COVID degree, I'm autistic and I have had a lot of friends backstab, betray and hurt me in the past.

Therefore, whilst I do have a lot of friends, none of them are actually at the university and that is a pain at times. Also, like everyone I had lost a lot of friends over the course of the pandemic either through death or lose of contact, and this was a major problem at the start of my Final Year.

Since this was the first time I had been on

campus since March 2020, at the very end of my First Year at university.

Therefore, I really wanted, needed to make a massive effort towards making friends this year. But not just friends for the year, friends for ages and for the rest of my life (well that's the theory anyway).

Now I admit this must sound very strange to a lot of people, but part of this is autism, part of this is how people have betrayed me in the past and part of it is just how difficult I find friendships. But I really struggle moving long-term attachments and I struggle even more investing a relationship beyond the time that I'm going to see a person for.

And no, I promise you I am not a horrible person for this thinking.

For example, during my first year at university, I lived in university accommodation and I really liked and became friends with two university friends, a French boy and an Italian girl, I had a lot of great nights talking to them.

However, because they were sadly returning to their own countries at the end of my first year, I sort of didn't want to commit or get too close because ultimately I knew they would leave me.

Therefore, in my Final year of university, I really wanted to get a great group of friends that I could get close with and keep for the long-term. And thankfully I have found those wonderful people.

How Your Final Year Is Great For Friendships?

During your Final Year at university, because no one just does a project alone, there are great ways to meet people during your Final Year Project and this is basically how I met all of my friends. Since I am very anti-social in lectures and I don't really talk to many people.

Anyway, when it comes to your final year project, you'll be doing the project with other people too. You all right up your own project but you get to do the same thing or similar things.

For example, on my final year project, there were four people. Me and my friend doing the EEG side of the experiment, another friend doing another variation of the experiment without EEG equipment and yet another one doing another variation of the experiment without EEG.

And there was a Masters' student that sort of popped in and out but didn't help out too much on the data collection side of things.

Anyway, as you can see I was working constantly with the great girl that was working with me on EEG and I got to work with two other girls too. They meant we could talk a lot, get to know each other and have fun and just become great friends.

And it is that becoming great friends that I really wanted from this year.

We've all laughed a lot, done a lot of things together and we're fully intending to stay in contact together. Which I definitely intend to do because these are all such great people.

Therefore, the entire point of this chapter is to say that your Final Year really is exactly what you make it. Be it academic or socially, if you want to make friends at university that could last forever then this is the year that you might very well be able to do it.

And as an autistic person and someone who has been treated poorly time after time by other people. I am so pleased that I have made friends and I have learnt to trust again and that is immensely powerful.

If you have had similar problems in the past then you might enjoy your Final Year a lot more than you imagine. Yet you need to be open-minded in the first place.

Anyone can storm in their Final Year, talk to people and make great friends, if they have the want to do it. Nothing in life happens by accident or without a little bit of work.

And making friends in your final year, now that is something that takes little work and even then the work is immensely enjoyable.

So go out, have fun and make new friends that might last a lifetime.

WHY REVISING STATISTICS IS A GOOD IDEA?

The great benefit of reading and listening to someone who has already done their Final Year at university is that you get to learn from their mistakes, and you get to see what they would have found helpful. This is certainly one of those chapters.

Since I will talk more about this in the next section of the book but me and the girl I was working with on my Final year project, we both struggled when it came to the statistics.

I struggled because I hadn't done stats for two years, because I did a one-year placement and then I hadn't looked at stats during the course of my Final Year either.

In addition, there were a lot of changes in psychology statistics since the time that I started my degree and my Final Year, because it was during my second year that the psychology world shifted towards R Studio. You know that wonderful little piece of computer software that requires you to learn it, know how to do it and requires you to code.

Now the problem was that my original cohort had never learnt R Studio because we were taught SPSS. And even though there were meant to be sessions so the placement students could learn R Studio, the Psychology Society is useless so they didn't have these sessions.

I never learnt R Studio so that is certainly a task for the summer.

Thankfully, we were allowed to use SPSS because stats is stats at the end of the day and even though, R Studio is what you need for the psychology job market, SPSS is still very easy to use for psychology coursework.

Nonetheless, the same problem still came back to us, the girl I was working with had never used SPSS, because her degree was on R Studio. And well, my stat knowledge was at least two years old and I didn't remember much of it.

Overall, this led to a hell of a lot of researching, frustration and laughter between us. We were hopeless, we really needed to focus and we needed to get down in the weeds of what we needed to do.

We bought in our old textbooks, our old notes and watched a lot of YouTube videos about how to do different bits and pieces. Thankfully, we both managed it in the end and we both got good grades.

Yet take it from me and my friend, definitely revise statistics for your final year, because not everyone is a perfect statistics student. Some people might find stats really easy, but other people don't.

Therefore, if you take anything away from this book definitely revise stats earlier on, you will be thanking me later and you will certainly be able to enjoy your data analysis and project a lot more if you get this nightmare of a topic out of the way.

Revise your stats and you might be able to live a much happier life come March time.

Now that we know what you need to think about and do before you start your Final Year, let's see how a Final Year Project works and what you can learn about my own personal experiences.

This is going to be a lot of fun.

PART TWO: FINAL YEAR PROJECTS

THIRD YEAR SURVIVAL GUIDE

INTRODUCTION TO FINAL YEAR PROJECTS AND REMEBERING YOUR SUPERVISORS ARE THERE FOR YOU

Kicking off the brilliant second section of the book and the real meat of the book, we're now going to turn our heads towards the Final Year Project that every single student I have ever met finds scary first of all, and some students even hate it towards the end of the year.

In this next section of the book, I'll be explaining, exploring and giving you some unofficial tips about the Final Year Project and its different sections. The entire point of this part of the book is to make sure that you have an idea about what to do, you know what mistakes to avoid and how to enjoy this Project.

Because I promise you, if you have the positive mindset and how that enjoyment is possible then your Final Year Project will be immensely fun.

How Does The Final Year Project Work?

Of course, I need to caveat this entire chapter and book by saying that obviously everything in this book is just based on what I had to do and in my own experience. Your university might require you to do something different, might have different names for sections or in the future, the technology might have changed so much that some of this isn't applicable anymore.

I'm not sure on the last part, I doubt it but I just wanted to add it in case it happens.

Also, originally I wasn't going to add in a copy of my Final Year Project in the back of the book without the data and references. Since I didn't think that would be relevant but then I realised that the book was really missing something without it.

So if you want to see a Final Year Project that got a high 2:1 is done then you can check it out in the back of the book. That way some of the things I talk about might make a little more sense.

Therefore, after you have picked your Final Year Project and your supervisor in your second year, the basic overview of the year is that you will have a meeting with your project group and then the following will happen:

- Expectations will be set.
- Write up your introduction
- Do data collection
- Do data analysis

- Write up the methods
- Write up the results
- Write up the discussion, conclusion and abstract
- Submit

Ah, it really does all sound so simple as I write it out but it isn't. It seriously isn't and that's why I'm going to be exploring some of these sections in this part of the book.

I won't really talk about your introduction because that's just a summary of the current literature and you justifying why your study is needed and why you're looking at what you're looking at.

In addition, I won't talk about the Pre-Registration assignment and the other piece of coursework I had to do as part of this module, because there isn't a lot I can say about this and I'm somewhat sure this is something only my university does for now, so it wouldn't be that useful to you.

However, what I will briefly mention is what happened in over the summer and early part of my Final Year from the standpoint of my Final Year Project.

We all got our assignments to projects in early June and then in July we all had a meeting about what the project involved and we could sort of meet each other. But as everyone knows, how well can you actually meet people over Zoom?

Then over the summer we were given a whole bunch of readings to look at, we were given the option of writing up our introduction and we had another meeting or two before the Final Year started in late September.

Of course, no one did this but I have to admit this was immensely valuable to me and the others, because we got a massive head start on our Final Year Projects compared to other students. And it was so great to understand what we were doing sooner rather than later, as well as it was good to "meet" people.

Granted I completely forgot their names, who they were and I didn't really pay attention to anything about the people I was working with in my Final Year, but that's just the bad stuff about Zoom.

Afterwards, during Freshers Week, we all went into the lab and the data collection side of our Final Year Project was explained to us. It was fun, we got to understand how everything worked and we got to finally meet each other, that was wonderful.

Then the university year started and after a few more practice sessions, we made sure to start our data collections weeks (and probably months) ahead of other Final Year Project students on other projects.

I'll talk about the fun of data collection in the next chapter, because there were challenges but it was immensely fun. Remember, having a positive mindset is important.

<u>Remember Your Supervisors Are There For You</u>

Personally, I always wanted this section later in the book but I needed to put it here because this is something you need to remember throughout the entirety of your final year. Your Final Year Project supervisor is your academic advisor for the year meaning definitely take advantage of them if you have any psychology, university or any other questions.

These are knowledgeable people that want to support you, get to know you and they want to see you thrive.

Therefore, if you are ever struggling then ask them a question, get help, just do not suffer in silence. My supervisor was brilliant this year and he helped me more than he could ever realise, so please, I want you to have the same advantages as I did.

Don't be afraid to ask questions if you need help. When it comes to something as important as a Final Year Project, there is no such thing as a stupid question and if there is then you might silently swear at your supervisor behind their back.

Just remember this year that your supervisor is there to support you, help you and make you thrive, if you put the work in obviously.

Once you remember that and actually follow that advice, I promise you your Final year gets a hell of a lot easier.

WHAT IS DATA COLLECTION, WHY IS IT IMPORTANT AND WHY I LOVED IT?

Moving onto our first major topic when it comes to your Final Year Project, data collection is arguably one of the most important parts and it is normally what you start off doing as soon as possible in your Final year.

Of course, this is very much based on your own project, what you're doing and what you are studying but this is still a great chapter because it gives you a chance to see what I got up to, how to have a positive mindset and most importantly how to have fun during this time.

Since I can promise you your data collection, especially if you're working with participants, is the most fun you will have during your Final Year Project.

I admit that my project was great for this, because it was lab-based, I got to interact with participants and I saw them for basically two weeks.

This allowed me to get to know them more and I got to have great conversations with them as well.

For the sake of context, the data collection part of my project involved 7 sessions, and this does require some explanation.

On the Monday to Friday every day of the first week, a participant would have to learn 8 Japanese symbols using a retrieval-based learning task. Then on the Monday and Friday there would be an EEG cap fitted to them so we could measure brain activity.

Afterwards on the following Monday, there would be what is known as a Refresher session so the participant gets to see all 40 Japanese symbols again using the same Retrieval-Based learning task as before.

Finally, on the Friday of the second week, we tested them using a range of methods to see how many of the Japanese symbols they remembered.

Overall, that was a grand oversimplification of the study and I got to see participants for two weeks.

That was my data collection so each week we got 6 participants to go through the motions, complete the experiments and ideally we needed at least 30 EEG pieces of data and then the same for behavioural data. The testing on the final Friday was behavioural data.

Your data collection will likely look extremely different because normally if you do a lab-based study you see the participant once and that's it. You don't get to develop relationships like we did with our participants and you don't get to know anything about them. Like their Christmas plans in December.

If you end up doing a thematic analysis-based project then I feel sorry for you. If you end up doing a project involving an online survey and you just analyse the results, then again I feel sorry for you.

Granted I know that some students like the analysis of online surveys but to be honest, that just isn't me. I like talking and interacting with participants and just having fun with them. You really can have a lot of laughter, conversations and joy with lab-based participants.

That is something you might want to think about when deciding on the project you want to do.

Why Did I Love Data Collection?

Another reason why I really liked data collection was because participants are the best, but also the worst at times, and like in real research (because your Final Year Project is real research) things will always go wrong.

We had some brilliant participants and because of ethical guidelines and data protection laws I cannot say their names, but me and the girl I was working with, we had a mental list of participants that we really, really liked working with.

Not always because they were brilliant at the task with one notable exception, but because they were just great people. For example, one woman that was sensational was good because she moved heaven and earth to make sure she could remain part of our study when she found out she had double-booked on the Friday.

She had booked to go home for the weekend and her dad was going to pick her up after work, and she had booked a 3 pm EEG with us.

It was fun and good that she moved her day around so we didn't lose data and she didn't lose out on her credits.

That's what I want to mention here. Sometimes participants are great people that want to help you and go the extra mile because they realise they are going to be in your shoes in very short order.

On the flip side, you have some right nobs, never be a nob everyone, because you will get participants that don't show up, are argumentative and swear at you. These were only ever the minority of cases but you will notice an uptick towards the end of term because in my university's experience, the good students get all their credits at the beginning of the term. Whereas all the bad and "lazy" students leave it until the end of the term and that's when the problems appear.

I will admit that I rather liked no shows because it meant I got to write sensationally cold, formal and funny emails that made my Final Year Project group laugh.

Here's one below:

"Dear X,

I regret to inform you that due to you not turning up for your session today at 1:30 pm as part of the Japanese Symbol study, you are no longer part of the study. This was a 7-part study and you needed to attend each of the sessions.

Therefore, please do not come in for any of the other sessions and I have deducted 12 credits from your RPS account per School policy.

In the future, it is best if you let researchers know if you're going to be late because things happen and we understand that, but you did not reply to emails so we have to terminate you from the study.

Good luck with your future studies and world languages degree,

Connor."

In you couldn't tell I do enjoy these sort of emails.

Anyway, as a researcher, you will meet some great and awful participants but the vast, vast majority of participants are wonderful and they really help to make the Final year Project a lot of fun.

In addition, when it comes to your data collection, there will be problems and that's okay. There was a good, well-founded reason why our study was deemed *cursed* by my supervisor and his PhD student. Something always went wrong and if I was pay-as-you-go I would be bankrupted by my phone bill.

Me and the girl I was working with really needed to call him often when something went wrong. Not because me and my friend were thick or stupid, it is because we tried to fix things ourselves but we aren't MATLAB or EEGGo64 experts.

Leading to us losing the first three weeks of our EEG data because no one realised that the EEG cable wasn't plugged into the computer. There were other EEG problems like when the girl I was working with and the Masters student helping us didn't press record on the EEG software.

I made some mistakes but after a ton of hard work and calling the University's IT support, we solved them. The standing joke was I rarely made mistakes, but when I did they were almost impossible to fix.

Therefore, once we realised that the EEG cable needed to be plugged in, we didn't realised that we were losing every other participant's data because the cable was plugged into the EEG equipment, but not the computer itself.

Or it was but the connection was bad.

Resulting in us having tons of behavioural data and only 23 out of maybe 50 EEG datasets.

That was annoying as hell but funny at the same time.

Also, all these problems did require a lot of panicking, rushing about and saying sorry to participants.

Seriously though, it was just all, part of the fun and it was the combination of participants and these problems that really made me enjoy data collection.

Returning To The Idea Of A Positive Mindset For Data Collection

I constantly hear that tons of my fellow students hated data collection, it was awful and it was the bane of their life. And I think part of it comes from their bad attitude towards it and they need a more positive mindset.

Since I believe because I went into data collection knowing I had to do it, I had picked a project that I wanted to do and I was open to the idea that this was going to be fun, I think that massively improved my experience of it overall.

That positive mindset helped me realise that I could be relaxed, I could be chatty and I could enjoy my time doing the experiment with the participants. Because I truly believe that life is way too short to do something you hate, so you might as well enjoy your data collection.

Your data will take months and months to collect so you better enjoy it otherwise those months are going to be hell for you. And believe me, when it comes to your Final year Project, you have a lot more hell-related things to experience before you press that delightful submission button.

As scary as the idea is, just try to enjoy your data collection, it is a lot more fun than you think and it can really make your Final Year your best year at university so far.

THE TRAUMA, THE CRYING AND THE JOY OF DATA COLLECTION

If you cast your mind back to earlier chapters of the book, I stressed the importance of making sure that you have revised stats, R Studio and whatever else you might need for psychology data analysis. This chapter is literally the reason why and let me tell you, this is honestly the most traumatic part of the Final Year Project.

Therefore, what I will do in this chapter is explain what happened with our data analysis and what me and the girl I was working with was doing and then I'll give you some tips and tricks, so you can avoid the sheer trauma me and my friend experienced.

Also, it is good to bear in mind that whilst me and my friend had to deal with EEG data and behavioural data. The vast, vast majority of people will only have to ever deal with behavioural data that you can "simply" format in SPSS or R Studio or whatever else you use.

As a result, data analysis started with a two-hour Zoom talk and demonstration about how to work the EEG data analysis software followed by an explanation of the behavioural data side.

Now I love the PhD student that was talking about it to us, he's great, but by God was this traumatic. If I was a very intelligent person I might have realised this was simply foreshadowing the next few weeks of my little life.

However, I seriously doubt anyone, any academic and any person designed to help us would have been able to give that two hour talk in a better way. It was just so much information, so much detail, so many steps about what to do when analysing EEG data.

And it was even worse that because the software used to analyse it doesn't work on my laptop, I couldn't even follow along with it. Neither could my friend and it was just a very long talk.

Afterwards me and my friend met up at university a few days later, we laughed about the talk and we both agreed that it was an impossible talk and the PhD student who was helping us did the best he could do. And I still firmly believe that no one could have given it better.

Then we tried to do the statistics, we tried to create the new variables that weren't in the excel or SPSS spreadsheet, but we couldn't.

Overall, me and my friend spent four long hours trying to solve the statistics problems we were having.

We watched YouTube videos, we watched old lectures and we looked through our stat notes from first and second year.

Four hours and we were no closer to solving this.

I think the clearest reason why this was happening was because R Studio was proving too problematic for her, and I had never used it or been taught it. And she had the exact same problem with SPSS, but SPSS is so much simpler.

Anyway, we called one of our friends in who is just sensational at stats, and we thought we had made progress but the meeting we had with our PhD student the next day proved otherwise.

He helped us thankfully.

Then the next two or three weeks (but it felt like a year) we were going backwards and forwards between me and my friend about the stats, what tests each of us needed to make sure we had the results to support what we wanted to look at, and more.

There was a lot of stuff going on.

And by the end of it, me and my friend were so damn happy to be done with the statistics. It was so long, so traumatic and it really proves why you need to know stats in psychology.

And that didn't even touch the trauma of the EEG analysis that I'm going to be talking about in the next chapter.

What Tips Would I Give You?

Firstly, the main tip is making sure that you revise your stats before you start data analysis, and I mean really revise them. I think if me and my friend had revised the stats and how to run different tests before we started then we would have been better off and the stress would have been dramatically lower.

Secondly, you need to work methodologically because even though we weren't making progress, it still felt like we were because we were planning each stage before we did it. This allowed us to make sure we were okay and we weren't making any silly mistakes by simply jumping into analysis we didn't understand.

Thirdly, I think you need to be kind to yourself because you don't know everything, and we all know students that think they're God's Gift to psychology, and they tend to be nobs anyway. Therefore, if you acknowledge that it's okay not to be experts in stats, it's okay not to know everything, and it's okay to ask for help then that will really help you when it comes to the data analysis.

I have to admit that whilst the data analysis part of the Final Year Project was the most traumatic part of the year, it was filled with laughter too. Me and my friend spent a lot of time together laughing, being annoyed at the stat software and we were helping each other.

I seriously couldn't have done the stats without her being there with me. She was amazing and it was nice that we were both as useless at stats as each other. I was more confident and proactive about the getting it done but it was still fun.

And again, a positive mindset about how the Final Year Project is fun and interesting certainly helps at times like this.

RESULTS, CRUNCH TIME AND DOING THINGS IN ADVANCE

Before we turn our attention to the writing up of the Final Year Project, I want to focus on the results themselves, the crunch time towards the end as the deadline approaches and why you seriously, seriously need to do things in advance because you just flat out never ever know what is going to happen in that damn final week.

<u>Results Can Take Time</u>

I fully admit that this both will be and not be a problem for every single psychology student reading this book. Since me and my friend we had to deal with EEG data and this is impossibly difficult to analyse. I'll save you all the long, boring details but because you basically need to do EEG analysis frame by frame, removing eye-blinks and frames with artifacts in and the sheer size of the files is massive. The problem is that each participant's EEG data takes two hours to go through.

My supervisor thankfully didn't want us to do all of it because it would have taken too much time. But considering my supervisor is immensely busy (and I mean I have no idea how his wife even sees him), this was always going to take a lot of time to get the EEG data analysis back to us for our Final Year Project.

That was just stressful towards the end because our project was due in on the Thursday, we got the values for the EEG data on the Tuesday.

Not fun. So not fun.

Equally, I'm mentioning this because even if you don't do EEG data, you still might be in a similar position because we only had the data to analyse early-on because we had started so early on our data collection.

If you don't start data collection very early then you might be pushing your luck with the data analysis later on. Granted the actual start date of your data collection isn't in your control, because of factors like supervisors, ethics committees and more.

However, my point is just be prepared for something to go wrong and that's why the other two sections in this chapter are so critical.

The Crunch Time

It honestly doesn't matter how organised, how focused or how well-planned your project is but at some point as the deadline approaches you will experience what I am calling the Crunch Time.

This is when you realise how close the deadline is and you realise you have tons left to do. I have never met a single university student that hasn't gone through this problem and I find it interesting.

I partly experienced it earlier on everyone else, not that I told them, because I always like to finish way, way before a deadline. For example, if there's an essay deadline for the 6th April 2023, I would like to get it done before the end of February.

As a result, Crunch Time is always stressful, concerning and oh boy, do you panic. You know how important the project is to your grade, you know how critical it is that you finish and you really know that there is a lot of pressure on you.

Just relax.

Of course that is easier said than done but this is where being methodological, calm and planning comes into this problem. If you realise and make notes about exactly what you need to do, effectively making a To Do List, then you're allowing yourself to notice that you actually hadn't got that much left to do.

Or you realise you really need to get on with it and you can break it down further into really easy to tackle pieces. For example, you might find it helpful that under the Subheading of your list, *Formatting Graphs,* you might want to write down a Figure Number so you quickly tick off each one.

Since graph formatting only takes a minute a graph so you can quickly see how much progress you're making.

I don't know what works for you but during

Crunch Time just be kind to yourself and I talk about this in the final section of the book anyway.

Doing As Much As You Can Before The Final Week

As you can probably realise, I don't like to leave things to the last minute and that I think is an absolute nightmare when that happens.

However, this Final Year Project was eye-opening in the fact that I basically had to work up until two days before the deadline. Some people I know were working up until the minute before the deadline.

Do not do that. That is dangerous.

Seriously don't want a late submission on something like this.

Anyway, the problem for the final week before submission was plentiful, because not only was I was waiting for the EEG data analysis to be done, but my nan was dying in hospital and she was meant to have died on the Saturday before the deadline. So me being the good grandson I was went up with my mum (my nan's estranged daughter) to say our goodbyes because it was the right thing to do.

Of course, family is a very complex business but there was a lot of shouting, arguments and disrespect as soon as we walked into the hospital room with my dying nan. So my mum said goodbye, I didn't and I just hated that.

She didn't die for another week but during deadline week I was constantly waiting for the phone call that would finally confirm that she was dead.

Not exactly ideal in deadline week.

However, thankfully because I always like to finish before deadlines I had gotten 99% of my Final Year Project done before the week of the deadline allowing me to get a lot of breathing space.

Therefore, what I'm saying is that it is an excellent idea for you to do things for your Final Year Project way before the deadline, because you just don't know what's going to happen. You don't know if something bad will happen, if your laptop will die, if you'll accidentally delete your work and so on.

Backing up your work is another great idea.

Overall, just prepare yourself, do things in advance and be kind to yourself then that will help you a lot in managing your Final Year Project.

Because the last thing I want for you is to be stressed, concerned and panicking over the project.

THIRD YEAR SURVIVAL GUIDE

WRITING UP THE PROJECT AND TAKING HELP

Whilst I could do a chapter on the statistics, results and the discussion sections of your project, I can't really do that because that will depend so much on your own individual project and your university will probably have a lot of great resources available to help you in these areas.

However, what I do want to focus on in this chapter is the actual write up of the project and how if there is any help offered to you, why you need to take it.

When it comes to the write-up, your word count might vary from mine but I had the word limit of 5,000 words. And to be honest, a lot of students think that is an impossible feat, it is flat out impossible to write 5,000 academically written words, but I promise you once you get into the "meat" of your project you will start to understand that isn't a scary amount.

In fact, you start to get scared of how little you

can actually write.

Personally, this was really hammered home to me when I started to re-read the Master student's project that we were given to help us understand the sort of things we were looking at, how the methods was done and the rest of it.

I have to admit that if there is a Masters student's project and the student themselves who has done the project before then it is definitely a good point of reference and it helps you to structure your response.

Of course, the first time I read it, I didn't understand it at all. As far as I was concerned it was just long, boring and filled with more concepts than I knew what to do with.

However, when it came to the writing up of the project, I did occasionally use it as reference material so I could understand how to better structure my sentences, my paragraphs and overall argument in the project.

It was really useful and helpful and a godsend.

I won't lie. The vast, vast majority of students will not get access to something like this, but I do recommend you read academic papers, academic literature reviews and more because they are the same sort of thing.

It is all about looking at professionally written academic texts and seeing how to apply their writing style and their methods of wording things, and then adapting all that knowledge into your own project.

Because come on, we all know how anal and

snobby academia is, and even if you misword one tiny little thing they deduct marks from you.

Academia is a nightmare at times.

In addition, when it comes to the writing up, you definitely need to be methodological like I've mentioned before because it can get overwhelming but if you simply plan out what you need to do, this makes it a lot easier.

As well as the upcoming chapters on being kind to yourself and other exam-related topics, actually do apply to this project too. There is no point allowing this project to consume your entire life, you stop doing things that make you enjoy life and more.

You have to get the project done but you need to balance your social and academic life really well.

Overall, I'll confess that the writing up part of the project can be intense at times. Yet if you plan social and relaxing time for yourself, you do as much as you can during your Final Year and you have a positive and fun mindset during the process. Then honestly, this is far, far from bad.

And when you get to the critical thinking part of your project, you can have a lot of fun with it. Since who doesn't love slagging off the research done by professionals and pointing out all their mistakes?

That can be a lot of fun.

<u>If Help Is Available Take It</u>

Something a lot of people don't know about me is that I don't really like bothering people or asking for help. A lot of that comes from my childhood and how people forced me to focus on becoming a very independent person and that has become a very important part of me.

On the other and, I will also admit that I am not perfect. As you've seen throughout this book, I have my own struggles, I am far from perfect when it comes to academia and I have struggled in the past with academic writing.

Therefore, whilst I have never ever done badly in this project and there haven't been any major, major problems that would have caused me to fail. There will always be room for improvement and a few issues that need to be reworded for clarity or something similar.

At my university, the majority of your feedback was gotten from the feedback form for a Pre-registration form that we had to write up as part of our coursework for this project. We got a lot of feedback but you could subtly ask very generic questions to your supervisors too.

Those generic questions were great and if you gone your supervisor completely alone then they *might* (emphasis on might) have answered more specific questions on your specific project.

Just saying that *might* have happened not that it ever did. It didn't.

Anyway, at my university, the supervisor have complete authority to look at your results to make sure they were correct, formatted correctly and the result section was perfect. It would be very hard otherwise to write up a good discussion if your discussion was based on faulty data.

I have to admit that looking over the results was helpful because it was good I knew everything was correct, formatted in the right way and I wasn't going to lose any marks for stupid reasons.

Also, you will be doing this in a group with other students under the same supervisor. You would all be doing your own projects, you would be looking at different things and you would all know what the project was like. So you could read each other's, make recommendations or give other people points.

I'll admit there is a "risk" here that you might accidentally copy each other or you might get a nob that steals something from you. That is a possible risk so actually, I would only do this with people you trust.

Or better yet, ask your non-psychology friends that are also doing their Final Year Project to read it, and you read theirs in return. You would both be doing the same thing more or less so it might be helpful to get a non-psychology viewpoint on your project.

This is very good considering modern day academic writing is meant to be understandable to non-experts in your area, and your second marker will be a non-expert anyway.

Therefore, what I am saying with this section is that help will always be available to you during your Final Year Project. You just need to realise that you need to take this, accept this and search out for help.

Due to your project will never be perfect, there will always be room for improvement and your supervisor will always be happy to help you within the rules that the university gives them.

The writing up part doesn't have to be scary, despite a lot of students going into this stage of the project with that mindset. I can promise you if you go into the writing up part calmly then it makes the journey of writing up everything a lot smoother, happier and it helps you more than you can ever know.

When I set out to write this book I had no idea this would turn out to be a mindset book more than anything else, but honestly, your Final year, half of it is a mindset battle.

I really do know that more than most.

MY OWN STRUGGLES AND THE RELIEF

To wrap up this Final Year Project section of the book, I want to tell you about my own struggles in my Final Year overall and then I want to tell you about the weird relief that every single university student finds whenever they submit their project.

And the relief goes for exams too.

<u>My Struggles During My Final Year</u>

Throughout the entire book, I have mentioned that I have had a lot of fun this year, I have laughed a lot, enjoyed my project and everything it involved. I've also enjoyed making brand-new friends even more.

However, that doesn't mean in any way that I haven't struggled this year in certain areas, and I'm telling you this for two main reasons. Firstly, I want you to know that I'm not superhuman and I am not cherry-picking what I put in this book. Secondly, I truly want you to know that if you struggle during your Final Year that is more than okay and you can still thrive despite struggles.

If you try and find a way to overcome these struggles.

As a result, my main struggle this year was my mindset and partly mental health surrounding grades and what I needed to get for my Masters.

I was so desperate, so excited, so eager to stay at my university for my Clinical Psychology Masters for reasons I explain in the next section of the book, that I really, really didn't want to fail.

Looking back, I actually had nothing to worry about because I got a 78 in my placement year but at the time I had no idea that factored into my overall degree classification, more on that in the Exam section of the book.

In addition, when I was in my first and second year I was terrible with essays and academic writing so I was fairly sure that I wasn't going to do any better. Thankfully because of my placement year working with a wonderful PhD student and a supervisor, I managed to improve my academic writing dramatically.

But when your mental health isn't that great anyway on certain days, getting bad grades doesn't help matters too much.

Since I got my first piece of coursework back at a 72 for a single short-answered question. So I thought that I had made it, I was good enough to do well and more.

Then we answered the rest of the short answer questions and I got a 55 for those three and my seminar report thankfully came back at a 65. Overall, I think I averaged out about a 65 for that module.

That's not too bad and I could sort of live with that because the average was more important.

Then I was really happy that I got my psychosis essay back with a 72. Which meant my essay writing jumped from a 52 to 72. I was seriously happy about that.

Then things went downhill a little, since I got a 55 in my Applied Psychology intervention proposal that was rather saddening because I had really enjoyed the topic and had poured my heart and soul into it.

Then a poster we needed to make resulted in grade of 58 and as you can imagine I was being really hard on myself because I knew at this rate I wasn't going to be doing anything too grand or exciting with my life.

I actually remember an extra bad Monday, two days before my first exam, and I was so down and I was basically calling myself a retard in my head, because I was so done with university. Since back then, it seemed like no matter how hard I tried, I just kept failing.

However, early May I got my critical review back at an 82 and another essay back at a 68, so I could finally accept that I wasn't going to fail my degree and I could continue on with my Masters in September.

Of course, I still focused extra hard on my exams

but the pressure was off a little.

Overall, I should have been kinder to myself, like there was no reason to call myself a retard, and I shouldn't have focused so much on the negative, but I really wanted this Masters at my university.

So in case you have similar struggles just know that things do get better, things can improve if you try and focus on making things better.

The Weird Sensation Of Relief

After I had submitted my project and actually the same goes for my exams, I realised that there was a massive sense of relief that washed over me. Since I was done, I didn't have a project consuming my life anymore and I was free to get back to my other projects.

Yet I also have to admit that there was a sense of emptiness because this project had consumed so much of my time, brainpower and passion for so long that I actually felt a little surprised that it wasn't in my life anymore. I didn't have to spend an hour or two or three on it a day and it was just so weird.

The same happened after my exams because I was done with my undergraduate degree. I didn't have to do anything else, I didn't have to revise anymore and I never ever had to focus on damn applied psychology ever again.

That was a great bonus because that intervention proposal turned me against that module very firmly.

Therefore, what happened was that after my last exam I did some work as a student ambassador later that night, and there was a comment made because a whole bunch of us had finished our Final Year Projects and more.

Then the staff member for Outreach mentioned something along the lines of *do you know what you've going to do with yourself now*. Interestingly enough I didn't know what she meant at the time and I didn't for ages, because I just thought I would go back to my writing, podcasting and more and dedicate more time to those projects.

And I did, but I also had the strange sense in the afternoons (when I normally worked on my revision or project) that I wasn't sure what to do with myself.

So I asked around, I asked my friends about how they found submitting their project and every single person I asked went through the same experience.

It is such a nice thing to actually experience but it is really weird and surprising at the same time, because you are basically free of your undergraduate degree.

After so many years you are finally free and that is a hell of a feeling to have.

PART THREE: THINKING ABOUT AFTER YOUR FINAL YEAR

THIRD YEAR SURVIVAL GUIDE

WHAT TO DO AFTER UNIVERSITY?

I'll definitely talk about this topic in more depth and from a personal perspective in the last chapter of this section but until then, this is a great chapter to help you understand what *is* possible after university.

***

The topic of this next chapter is sort of one of those horrible but very much needed questions that pops up in every university student's mind. As well as I can tell you from personal experience that it does change, so even if you're a brand-new university student who thinks they know exactly what they're doing after their undergraduate degree.

Please change your mindset slightly now to at least be open to the possibility of that not working out or you wanting to change your mind.

It is natural and a very, very real possibility.

But that could be both a bad thing, or an extremely positive thing!

What To Do After University?

What to do after university? Is a major question on the mind of most students. Especially if you're entering the final year of your bachelor's degree, so the aim of this post is to help make you aware of some of the options available to you. Not only does this allow you to start planning your future, but they'll be some questions too so you can find out if this choice is right for you.

Why Do You Need To Think About What To Do After University?

The most important reason to do this is because some of these options need you to do things in your final year. Therefore, if you know what you're aiming for after your degree, you can start to prepare and position yourself for this in the final year. For example, if you want a job after your degree, then looking at how to improve your employability is important.

Speaking of which.

Getting A Job:

After working for three (or however long your degree is) years, you might decide that you don't want to study for a Masters or PhD and instead you want to get a job. There is nothing wrong with this and the vast majority of students do this option.

Whether you get a job in your degree subject or in another sector entirely that is down to you. But because you have a degree, as far as employers are concerned, you are clever and you have a lot of transferable skills that might be useful to them. For example, critical thinking, analysis and evaluation skills would be useful to a very wide range of businesses.

In addition, even if you realise in your final year (or at any point for that matter) that you don't want to work in your degree subject area. Don't despair because your degree has still taught you a lot of valuable skills that employers want.

However, the only thing I would say against this option is where do you want to work?

Due to if you want to work in a science field then this option is not for you, technically. For example, if I wanted a psychology job then I would have to move onto a Masters and then probably a PhD to get a good psychology job. It's just one of the good things about the psychology job market.

Meaning if you want a job that requires a lot of education, this option isn't available to you. Unless you want to take a break from education then return to it so you can get your dream job.

Overall, getting a job and leaving education is a great option to consider.

Ascend To Higher Education:

Technically, you're already in higher education but we'll skip over that little detail (it should be higher-higher education).

However, if you don't want to get a job after finishing university, you could continue your education if your life allows it. As well as there will be future blog posts on the benefits and how do Masters and PhDs work.

Personally, this is the option I'll take because after my psychology degree. I'm intending to do a clinical psychology (mental health) Masters so I can continue my education. As well as whilst I might not do a PhD, there are still plenty of psychology jobs available with a Masters.

And this is what you need to consider when deciding what you want to do. You need to decide what will help you most and what will you enjoy. For instance, getting an everyday job outside psychology, I won't enjoy and by doing a Masters this will help me get the jobs I'm more likely to enjoy. As well as choose as a career.

On the whole, if you want or need to continue with your education so you can get the job you want in the future. Then doing a Masters, PhD or whatever your subject calls it (I know Law and accounting have some weird titles) can be a great idea.

Cannot Decide:

I know plenty of people who just cannot decide what they want to do after their degree. They don't know if they should get a job, continue with another degree or do something else entirely. Sometimes this is scary to them because they feel like they should know, because surely everyone knows.

So if this is you, then you aren't alone in these feelings.

Therefore, I would say what I've said in numbers

of blog posts. Focus on the long term and what you want to achieve (also known as goals), and if you don't know what you want to achieve, then sort that out first.

Once you know what you want for the long term, it will start to help you understand what you need to get there.

For instance, if you wanted to be an academic in, let's say, microbiology. Then you can start to think about what you need to do to achieve it. Like getting a Masters, PhD and getting research experience.

It's something to think about and of course these goals and long term focuses change. I think I've changed mine ten times since starting to think about psychology, but I know what I want to achieve now.

Overall, if you can't decide what you want, then look at your goals and go from there.

Conclusion:

As I (and thousands of other students) start my final year in September, I know lots of people will be scared by this topic. But hopefully after reading this blog post, you'll start to have some awareness about the options available to you after you leave university.

Finishing university doesn't have to be a step into the darkness and unknown. It just has to be something you'll enjoy and want to do for years to come.

And that's critical.

Because once you lose the enjoyment and fun in something, what's the point of doing it for another

few decades?
>There isn't.
>Just bear that in mind and you'll be fine.

WHY DO A MASTERS DEGREE?

Continuing with our look at what you can do after university, in this chapter we're going to explore what exactly is a Master's Degree, why is it useful and why you might want to do one. I definitely think that all of these chapters looking at different options are critical to read because they really do give a lot of breath and depth into possible options you can do after university. And as I mention in the introductions for these chapters, you start to get an understanding of how difficult it is to find easy to understand and simple information about these options.

Basically, I would have loved to read these chapters at an early stage of my university journey.

I hope they help you and maybe even inspire you a little.

Why do A Masters Degree?

With me starting my final year at university in a few months, I wanted (and needed) to start thinking about what I wanted to do after I graduate. I know I've covered *What To Do After University?* In another blog post, but now I wanted to focus on doing a Masters Degree specifically. Yet in case you're unsure whether this is a good thing or not for you, I'll explain the benefits, the drawbacks and my own thinking process towards a Masters Degree.

What Is A Masters Degree?

Just so everyone is on the same page, a Masters Degree is the type of degree you do after a bachelors but before a PhD, and yes I know that was extremely oversimplified. But that's the simplest definition of what it is, and I'll be defining a Masters Degree through the post as its benefits are rather unique compared to a Bachelor's.

However, just like a Bachelor's you can do a Masters of the Arts or Sciences, with Masters of Sciences focusing on scientific research, rigour and methods.

What Are The Benefits of Doing a Masters?

More Specialisation:

This is definitely one of the greatest benefits in my opinion about doing a Masters. Since they allow you to specialise in your degree subject and become more of an expert in that little (or large) area.

Then this specialised knowledge can be very useful in allowing you to get access to even higher levels of education and it allows you to become a lot better in a specialised area.

For example, at the moment, I study psychology

as a Bachelors. Therefore, in a way, I know a lot of topics within psychology at a good amount of depth, so I have a good breathe and depth of knowledge.

However, a masters degree would allow me to deep dive into clinical psychology (just think mental health) and really focus on that fascinating area. Allowing me to become a lot more knowledgeable about a very wide range of topics within that area.

Personally, I really like the sound of that because I am passionate about that subfield and I do want to learn more.

Therefore, if there's an area of your degree subject that you want to explore and increase your expertise in. Then a Master's degree might be a great idea for you.

Access To Higher Paying Jobs:

Now this is a major reason why I want to do a Masters, because one of the reasons why I chose to do a psychology degree (besides from how interesting it was), was because you cannot do anything in the psychology job market without a Masters degree at the least.

Now I know that might scare, concern or worry some people, but I like it. Since it means you'll only be competing against other degree educated people (at least that's the lie I tell myself to pretend getting a job will be easier).

Therefore, there are plenty of job markets, especially in the sciences, that require you to have an advanced degree before they will even consider your job application. As a result, if you want to work in one of these fields then this is a very good reason to consider doing a Masters.

As well as even if you do want to work in a sector that doesn't require you to have a degree. It could still be a good idea because it might give you an extra leg up in the job application process, but that depends on the employers and whatever job you go for.

Drawbacks To Doing A Masters:

However, as much as I love the idea of doing a Masters. I suppose I better try to keep this balanced, so here are the potential downsides of doing a Masters degree.

Another Year Out of Work:

Personally I didn't know this was a reason against it, because I believed students would actually see that as a benefit. But it turns out lots of people see this very much as a negative, so we need to explore this drawback.

After talking to different people over the past few months, I realise that this drawback comes down to a few different things.

Firstly, people are concerned that after spending the past three or four (or however long your degree is) years at university. They might be better off starting work, increasing their employability and getting out into the real world.

Personally, I do completely understand that. But as I said before a Masters degree could make you even more employable depending on your desired job, and you can still increase your employability whilst studying. That's what part-time jobs are for.

Secondly, people are concerned about the cost, the debt, etc. Which I'll address below, but if you're living in the UK then it very arguable that the maintenance and tuition fee loans are basically free money. But I cannot comment on how it works for other countries, especially the US.

Finally, without realising it, they're lying to themselves that they want to continue in education. I have seen this a fair amount of times where people are telling me they want to do a masters but X, Y and Z are stopping them. Then after a while, I manage to get it out of them that they don't really want to do another degree.

And that's fine.

There is absolutely nothing wrong with just having a bachelors degree. That's still amazing.

Yet I know there are normally family, personal or other reasons why people don't like to admit that they don't want to continue, and I'm afraid that is something you definitely need to deal with yourself. There's no advice whatsoever I can offer there to help you.

Cost:

I'm actually really glad I did this blog post because there's a very strong myth going around universities that you only get 4 years of government funding in the UK. But I just did a bit of research and thankfully UK students can apply for postgraduate funding, so that's thankfully no longer a factor for me.

Anyway, I do know that not all students have those luxuries, especially amongst our international audience (Granted some non-UK students have to pay a few hundred, not thousands of their currency for their degree. I wish that was an option here).

Therefore, if you are concerned about the cost of a Masters or another type of postgraduate study. Then I would unofficially recommend you look at possible scholarships, bursaries and loans that might be able to help you out.

I know that money and the cost of university is never an easy topic, but it is still a factor we must all consider.

Conclusion:

I'm really looking forward to the idea of doing a Masters degree, because I do want to become specialised in clinical psychology and deepen my knowledge on the subject. As well as I do want to be able to possibly go after those higher-paying jobs.

However, I know not everyone wants that, especially when we consider it's another year out of work and the cost of the degree itself, and that's fine. You don't need to have a postgraduate degree.

Just think about your options, what's right for you and your situation, and you should be fine.

At the end of the day, just do what makes you happy.

HOW MASTERS DEGREES WORK?

Now we all understand why you might want to do a Masters degree, we now need to look at how do they work. Due to you'll quickly find they work very differently compared to undergraduate degrees, so understanding the difference could be a critical factor in helping you to determine if this is something you want to do or not.

How Do Masters Degrees Work?

Originally this blog post was meant to be a very nuanced look at how Masters degrees work, and I planned to look at the main differences between them and undergraduates degrees and things like that. But I was talking to the editor of this blog because he's done a Masters degree, and I very quickly realised that wasn't going to work because I hadn't known how many types of Masters there were. So I had to zoom out a little, so if you want to learn more about the types of Masters degrees then this is definitely the post for you!

Also there will be a mini-interview at the bottom with someone who has actually done a Masters (and done very well at it too) for some tips.

Why Look At Different Masters Degrees?

If this was a blog that was dedicated to one subject area, for example psychology in the case of my podcast, then I could honestly do what I was going to do in the first place. But since this blog is aimed at students from so many subjects, I believe it's important to see what options you have as an undergraduate student.

Due to you might believe there is only one or two set options for you in your subject area, but as I found out the other day there are always options you didn't know about. That's why it's important to look at, so you know what is available to you, and you'll probably find the newly-discovered option might be a better fit for you.

Anything's possible.

What Are The Different Types of Degrees?

As this is a slightly more general post we aren't going to cover subject-specific Masters. For example, the specialised degrees from Law, Business, Art and other subjects. Instead we're going to cover the more general Masters which can be applied in a range of subjects.

For instance, the three most common Masters Degrees are Master of Arts, Master of Science and Master of Research. Which when grouped together I think sound like some strange military ranks, but these are the three I'll give an overview of for you.

What Is A Master of Science?

This I think is the most common to be because these programmes make up the majority of the options available in the social sciences, hard sciences, maths and engineering, and these are the subjects I'm more familiar with. As well as there are massive differences between a Master of Science and Arts.

In addition, a Master of Science focuses on the scientific method, logic and research with these degrees tending to be taught (meaning there are lectures, exams and similar things) over the course of one or two years depending on your subject.

I know from personal experience that clinical psychology degrees, which is what I want to do, is a Master of Science because it focuses on the scientific method, evidence and logic then applies it to mental health and related matters. As well as there are plenty of core modules that are taught to you to help you become more specialise in that area over the course of one year.

That's just one practical example of how a Master of Science is structured. As well as it is worth noting that the academic year for Masters students (regardless of the type) can be longer than undergraduate. Since some Masters are for an academic year (late September to Mid-June) or they can actually be twelve months.

Overall, if you're studying a subject where scientific rigour and research is the focus then a

Master of Science would be a very good idea to study. Since it allows you to deepen your research skills, become more specialised in a specific area and it helps you move on to the next stage. I'll talk more about that in a moment.

What Is A Master of Arts?

If my grandad was reading this he would have a heart attack at what I'm about to say next, but a Master of Arts and Science can be compared ever so slightly, at least until we get into the nitty-gritty.

Due to like Master of Science, a Master of Arts is a taught programme lasting one or two years and the arts, the humanities and some social sciences use Master of Arts. Yet that is where the similarities ends because whereas the Master of Science focuses on logic, the scientific method and research. This one does not.

As the Cambridge Dictionary defines this type of degree as **"an advanced college or university degree in a subject such as literature, language, history, or social science,"** so as you can see this focuses more on cultural and social aspects of the world that cannot be studied empirically.

This makes it perfect for students who want to learn languages, deepen their understanding of areas of history and discuss the work of Shakespeare. But this is far from perfect for other students that need to be research based.

Personally, I remember my cousin doing an MA and me and the rest of my family never actually understood what she did. We did honestly try to understand, but she kept saying she wanted to research aspects of the theatre. Yet we couldn't understand why she didn't do a Master of Science, so she had the empirical knowledge and research skills and then research this area. As well as even now as an undergraduate I try to talk to her about research and despite her completing her MA, I still know a lot more about research skills than her.

So... take of that what you will.

Overall, Master of Arts is a great choice for students who don't want to study science-based subjects, and want to study literature, language and history topics. Yet if science is for you, then definitely do a Master of Science. It would be a lot more useful.

The Differences Between A Master of Science And Art:

In addition to their different focuses, another critical difference between the two types is a Master of Art is what's known as a terminal degree. This means this is the highest level of achievement in a subject, and then a very, very small number of people might choose to do a PhD in the subject. But the vast majority of people do finish higher education with a Master of Art.

For example, a Master of Art in the French language is relatively common in certain circles, but a PhD (and therefore Doctor) of the French Language is exceptionally rare.

On the other hand, Master of Science students

tend to see a Masters as a stepping stone degree towards a PhD. I know that's how things are seen in psychology and others sciences as most of our jobs require a PhD, at least for the really good jobs.

What is A Master of Research?

This is basically the type of degree that shattered my ideas for this blog post because I only learnt about this type a few days ago at the time of writing. However, whilst I cannot say too much on this, the mini-interview at the bottom gives a bit more clarity on this type.

Therefore, a Master of Research applies to all subjects and the focus of the degree is researching an area you want to investigate. There are no deadlines for the course except the final deadlines where the project is due (at least in the research programme) and this type of Masters lasts for one to two years.

Moreover, this type can be divided into two further subtypes. Since a Master of Research can be strictly a research programme like the editor of the blog did, or it can be taught. This I've seen a little bit because there are degrees that focus completely on how to be a better researcher, probably in preparation for people who want to work in academia.

Conclusion:

I know I've probably given you a lot to think about but I want to help you by mentioning this: at the end of the day, there are positives and negatives to all types of Masters. One is not necessarily better than the other and they require intense focus and study. But each type of degree is better for a certain career goal.

Now you have this information in mind, bear in mind the type of Masters degree that will help you in your future career. That is where the critical decision and factors lay, so make sure you choose a degree that is in the best interest for your future.

<u>The Mini-Interview</u>

To give you even more interesting information about Masters degrees, I did a quick interview the other day with the great editor of this blog, Oliver Herdson for his experience of doing a Masters. I found it rather interesting to read, learn from and he gives some great tips.
Enjoy!

1. What was your Masters in?

My masters was a research programme (MSc-Research [MSc-R]). This means it is not a taught programme, so I had no lectures (other than stats). For my research, I elected to explore the role of sad music on emotion and depression.

2. What surprised you about your Masters compared to undergraduate degree?

The independence definitely surprised me. I also took on 3 final year project students (undergraduates) to supervise, and so I found myself surprised by my ability to take on this role.

3. How do you think a Masters compares to an Undergraduate?

My masters was very different, due to it being a research programme. You can think of it as a mini PhD. So, I had a lot more independence and a lot more responsibility. With no lectures or deadlines (apart from the final deadline), my organisation was my own responsibility. It's basically like taking on the final year project on a much larger scale.

4. What tips would you give students looking to do a Masters?

Definitely make the most of your time. Especially if you do a research programme, find some relevant volunteering or work experience to do on the side. For taught programmes, just keep on top of your own organisation and work load.

Quick Wrap-Up

The reason why I like this interview is because it really does highlight some important aspects to bear in mind when choosing a Masters degree, especially a Master of Research. As well as the interview helps with expectation setting and it highlights some of the skills you might need to start working on now so you're a little more prepared for it.

HOW DOES WORK EXPERIENCE BENEFIT UNIVERSITY STUDENTS?

Continuing with our look "preparing for after university", I really wanted to add in this blog post that I wrote for Active Class a while back. Since as much as no student wants to admit it (because come on, who wants to work for free?), work experience is an extremely powerful and valuable tool to put on your CV in later life. As well as having work experience in your chosen field does help you to standout more compared to other applicants that just *only* have the qualifications.

So definitely check out this next chapter and enjoy.

***

When it comes to employability and getting work experience lots of students don't see the point in it, so this next chapter focuses on the 5 main benefits of work experience and why students really need to do it.

You'll be surprised at the amazing benefits doing some work experience can have, so definitely check out this next chapter.

How Does Work Experience Benefit University Students?

In this increasingly competitive world, it is becoming harder to stand out in the job market and this is where work experience comes in. Because employers generally prefer people to have experience when they apply for jobs. So, it's important to consider How Does Work Experience Benefit University Students?

5 Benefits of University Work Experience

Taste of A Future Career

One of the many reasons why I picked to do a placement year (year of work experience) was because I wanted to explore what it was like to work in psychology. Therefore, I'm working with a great team in September 2021 to conduct some research.

This will allow me to see if I enjoy and I can see myself working in research for the rest of my life.

Personally, I would prefer to find out what I don't like about working in psychology now, compared to finding out after I've found a *proper* job that I hate it.

Overall, this is one reason why work experience is great to do because it allows you to see what you want to do in the future. Because you might find out you thought you loved Clinical practice, but after your work experience you realise you hate it.

Learn Beyond The Classroom

As great as lectures and textbooks are, they can only teach you so much. The rest of the skills you need you have to learn in the real world, and you can't do that without experiencing your degree in the real world.

Therefore, work experience is great for allowing you to develop skills you learn about in the classroom, but you don't get to apply.

Another point to add is in textbooks, they can describe a particular skill but it isn't until you have to use it in the real world that you realise how the skill actually works.

For example, in clinical psychology, we're told a lot about active listening and it sounds easy enough. But in the real world it isn't as easy as it sounds.

Meaning experience can help you familiarise yourself with how your degree works in the real world. Sometimes this can surprise you because the theory says one thing, your experience says another. But isn't that the fun of learning?

On the whole, getting work experience is great because it allows you to develop the skills you learn about in the classroom and turn the theory into practical knowledge.

Being Paid Is A Good Feeling:

Whilst this doesn't apply to all work experience because when I was applying to my placement there weren't many paid placements and generally work experience is unpaid. But I don't mind that necessarily because my thinking is if I get the experience now then this makes me more employable in the future. Meaning I'll hopefully make more money in the long term.

Of course, your circumstances might be different and I'm fairly sure if you hunted high and low you might be able to find some paid work experience.

However, if you do get paid work experience, this can be a great feeling as it allows you to work in the field you love, get the other benefits we've discussed, and you get to make some money too. Which is always good!

<u>Increased Employability</u>

Our final point we've preluded to throughout this blog post but I want to say it explicitly- work experience can equip you with skills and experiences that lots of people don't have.

For example, my placement year in research will help me develop my skills in researching a real-world setting. Other students in my year they'll have research experience from their degree but not necessarily in a real-life setting.

If you studied medicine and you got work experience at a Doctor's Surgery, you would have real-world experience and skills that I don't think many other students would have.

Overall, work experience can be great for increasing your employability because you will have some great skills and experiences that you can draw on in your future work.

Conclusion:

Whether you're actively looking for work experience or you're just interested in the idea, I hope you've found this useful. Work experience can have some great benefits from skill development to learning new things to increasing your employability. I hoped you learnt something.

Have a great day!

PREPARING FOR AFTER UNIVERSITY

To finish off this penultimate section of the book, I want to expand on the last few chapters because as great as those chapters were, they didn't have many real-world examples. That is the point of this final chapter because I want to explain in some detail what me and my friends are doing next year after our Final Year.

This will help you to see there is more than one option and way to do things after you finish this year.

You Could Stay At Home And Work Or Get Experience

I wanted to start off with this one because I know that whilst I always say that a psychology degree is "useless" without a Masters, I don't want everyone to think that you have to do a Masters even if you don't want to.

Since the girl that I was working with to do my Final year Project, she wants to become a neuropsychologist working with children, so she would become an educational neuropsychologist in the end. Therefore, she clearly needs a Masters but it isn't possible at the moment.

And just as a note for our international readers, in the UK, to become a clinical neuropsychologist (which is what she wants to become), you need to do a clinical psychology Masters, then do a Doctorate of Clinical Psychology, get two years of experience as a fully qualified clinical psychologist before doing another more specialist degree in clinical neuroscience.

The main reason why she can't do this at the moment is because she lives on the south coast of England and there aren't any good clinical psychology Masters in her area. Meaning she would have to move out from her home and live in another city, exactly like what she has been doing for the past three years at university.

Yet that requires money and she doesn't have any left after paying for her accommodation for the past three years.

As a result, she wants to go back home, live with her parents and work her job. She hopes to get work experience with children and other clinical populations so she can at least start on the road to becoming a clinical psychologist. Then when she has the money she'll move again to get a clinical psychology masters.

As well as considering how you need years of clinical experience working with in your four clinical settings (learning disabilities, working aged adults, retired people and child and adolescent), getting work experience is what she needs anyway.

Overall, I wanted to highlight her story because it's important to realise that you need to do what is great for you and your life circumstances. Also, you might not be ready to do a psychology Masters *now* but you might be in a good position in the future.

Just think about what is right for you and your life and then, and only then make the decision for what you want to do after university.

Do A Masters At A Different University

I have to admit that I do admire my two friends that are going to University College London next year to do a neuropsychology masters specialising in strokes. Due to UCL is a brilliant university, they're moving again and it does sound like an interesting course.

Yet I will admit that £20,000 a year for accommodation is beyond stupid. I have no idea how her parents are even paying for that. Another reason why I personally avoid studying in London.

Therefore, this is a great option to talk about, because you really don't have to stay at your current university. In fact, I was once told when I was planning to be a lot more adventurous than I turned out to be, that it is a good point if you don't stay at the same university forever. Since it shows to other academics that you haven't become institutionalized.

Of course when I was told that I had no idea

what that meant, but I think it means when you become engrained or accustomed to how a single university works, thinks and does things. Definitely not ideal.

Anyway, if you want to do a psychology Masters then look around, you don't have to stay at your current university and you can always follow friends if that's what you're into.

At the end of the day, when it comes to choosing what you want to do after university, you have to make sure it is what you want. If you want to do a Masters, that's brilliant. If you want to do a Masters at a different university or in a different country, that's brilliant too. If you want to not want to do a Masters, that's great too.

You just need to be open-minded and determined enough to choose what *you* want to do after university and make sure that whatever you pick helps you achieve your end goal.

<u>You Could Stay At Your Current University</u>

Moving onto yours truly, after my undergraduate, I've decided to stay on at my current university to do my clinical psychology Masters. I chose this for both academic and personal factors.

Firstly, in terms of academic reasons, I chose to stay at the university because it is a brand-new course and it is meant to have revolutionary modules that no other university in the UK offers. And yes, I am a real sucker for marketing at times.

In addition, I know the academics, I know how

good the university is and I know where I fit into the university eco-system so I am more than comfortable there.

When it comes to personal reasons, as an autistic person, I don't like change, I like to have some stability and constantly moving every few years doesn't help that and I want to form long-term relationships and friendships with other people. Something that constantly moving doesn't help with either.

Furthermore, I really like the university and I'm comfortable there so I don't want to move. Also, driving there is so easy so it isn't difficult to get to and I get to live at home so my accommodation costs are basically nil. Which is absolutely perfect as far as I'm concerned.

Moreover, I have my Outreach Ambassador job which I love, it's fun, easy money and I'm really valued and liked by the department. It was quite funny seeing their reaction to me saying I wanted to continue my Outreach job. They basically bit my hand off.

On the whole, there are a lot of personal and academic reasons why you might not want to change universities for your masters, and you might just want to stay where you are. That's okay. I want to stay at my university because I am honestly comfortable there, I have great relationships with other students and academic staff and the course sounds great.

And that's perfectly okay because this is what *I*

need, it might not be what you need after your undergraduate degree.

Just explore your options, have fun and do what is best for *you* and not anyone else.

PART FOUR: EXAMS AND MORE ON FINISHING YOUR FINAL YEAR

THIRD YEAR SURVIVAL GUIDE

INTRODUCTION TO EXAMS IN YOUR FINAL YEAR

Moving onto the final section of the book, I wanted to write this little introduction to exams because sadly, no matter how well you try to pick your optional modules, chances are your compulsory ones will have exams attached to them. Because universities are evil.

Therefore, to make sure that you're prepare for them and know how they're going to work, I've added a lot of chapters taken from very popular and highly praised blog posts that I've done over the years.

Also, I'm sharing more up to date stuff right now with you all. Then towards the end of the section, I'll mention some more thoughts about your Final Year as we wrap up this really fun book.

<u>Why You Need To Know Exactly How Your Exams Work?</u>

When I say this I'm not really talking about your

exams themselves, in terms of whether they're online, how long they are and what topics they cover. That is all critical to know as well and believe me, you absolutely have to know that information so you can plan effectively.

However, a wonderful little trick that I discovered during my Final year is how your academic grades for the past few years are weighted. We all know that your first year at university doesn't count at all towards your final degree classification but your second and third year do.

And in case you're like me, your placement year or year abroad also accounts and that was a great thing for me.

Since earlier in the book I mentioned that my second year was barely good enough to make sure I was on my placement year (you needed 60 and my average that I calculated was 61) so to say I was concerned at the beginning of this year was an understatement.

Nonetheless, because the weighing at my university was 50% for your final year, 30% for your second year and 20% for my placement year. That gave me a lot of breathing room, not that I realised that at the time.

As a result of me getting a 78 in my placement year, I managed to workout that as long as I got a 2:1 I will be okay in my final year and my overall degree classification. I wish I had realised this sooner so I was a little more relaxed throughout my entire year but at least I knew before my exams.

Overall, I really do encourage you to find out everything you can about your exams because this information could definitely help you, your stress levels and your general happiness during this time of exams.

And then you are free from university.

I have to admit, and you will probably doubt me until you've finished your exams, but this is a very weird feeling to have, because you have no more exams, no more coursework and no more Final Year Project. You are completely done with university and I know some students struggle with that first week after their exams because they don't know what to do with themselves.

And that is a brilliant feeling and situation to be in after the last three years of your life.

THIRD YEAR SURVIVAL GUIDE

HOW SHOULD UNIVERSITY STUDENTS PREPARE FOR EXAM SEASON?

Preparation in life really is everything and that is still extremely true for university and exams. If you aren't prepared for your exams, then guess what, you'll probably do bad or worse than if you were prepared.

But how do you prepare yourself?

That's the focus of this next chapter.

How Should University Students Prepare For Exam Season?

With the exam season only two or three months away, I cannot encourage you enough to start preparing yourself now. Therefore, when the exam season does start you are more prepared and it is a lot less likely that you'll get overwhelmed. So please expect plenty of useful tips in today's blog post.

How To Prepare For The Exam Season?

The simplest way to start preparing for the exam season is by starting to look at what exams you actually have. As well as sometimes you can be extremely smart about your exams, because sometimes you're able to minimize the number you have.

For example, as I write this post, I've just chosen by final year modules and thankfully there were more than enough interesting modules to choose that didn't have any exams. Of course, this might not be available to you, or you might do better in an exam compared to coursework. We are all different and you need to do what is right for you.

Therefore, you need to look at your exams so you know how many you need to prepare for, but you need to double check the details of the exams too. For example, during my second year, lots of my exams were different to each other. Some of them were open book, others were closed and the rest were multiple choice questions.

This sort of "deeper" understanding of your exams will really help you plan and prepare for them.

For instance, if you have five exams. Three of them were open book (meaning you can have a textbook open next to you) but the other two were closed book exams with two essay questions each. Then that is extremely important to factor in since you technically have more to revise in the essay exams compared to the open book ones. Considering in the essay exams you need to know all your citations and references off by heart, that is slightly less needed in the open book exams.

Anyway, all this will depend on your own exams and how they work. I do not envy law and accounting students. Their exams sound hard!

<u>Create A Revision Plan</u>

I know you've probably been told that millions of times and I know it can get extremely tiring but it is important. As well as when you factor in the importance of knowing your different exams then a revision plan can get very effective.

Therefore, all you need for that is create a few sessions in your busy university schedule that drops completely in the exam season to start revising your different modules. And to be honest, the reason this post is early and before the exam season is simple.

Start revising before the exam season!

That will give you plenty of time to see what you know, what you need to revise and improve on.

Then if you need to get the extra help then this buffer between you starting early and the exam season gives you the time to get it.

For example, let's say you gave yourself ten hours a week to study (do not take that as advice) and you have five exams to study for. Theoretically that means you have two hours a week for each exam, but you might not need that.

I know if I was doing this, I wouldn't need that long to study for a clinical psychology exam since I know it fairly well due to my podcast and other activities. But I know cognitive (mental processes) psychology a lot less well because it is a bit more complicated, so I might spend an hour on clinical psychology and three on cognitive.

That is why knowing your exams is so important, and this sort of flexibility needs to be put into your revision plan. As at the end of the day, you need to create a revision plan (and actually do it) that will help you as much as it can.

Then I recommend you find out what revision techniques work for you as well. There's no point in you using a technique because it is *"the right way to revise"* if it isn't working for you.

Conclusion:

This post really has scratched the surface of a very important topic that will be explored in future posts. But I really do recommend you start revising early, I know it doesn't sound fun but it is helpful, and I know whenever I have started something early I am really grateful I did that.

It definitely prevents all the stress of working right up to a deadline!

Therefore, start early, create a revision plan and revise effectively for you.

The exam season doesn't have to be scary, and those three things can definitely help you avoid the fear.

BEING KIND TO YOURSELF DURING EXAM SEASON FOR UNIVERSITY STUDENTS

When it comes to university exams no one ever thinks of this critical topic that really helps your mental health.

Therefore, I highly recommend reading this chapter even if you are perfectly fine with exams, because even if this chapter doesn't help you specifically it might be invaluable to a friend or family member.

And I think everyone will find this perspective very fresh, interesting and different.

<u>Being Kind To Yourself During Exam Season For University Students</u>

With the exam season coming ever closer, it is always a good idea to go over the basics. Like, the revision timetable, make sure you start revising early and revision techniques. That is all well and good but there is a critical factor that so many students miss out on and it can lead to devastating consequences. That is not relaxing and making time for yourself. So in this blog post, I'll explain why it's important, how to do and most importantly, how to find a balance.

Why Is Being Kind To Yourself During Exam Season Important?

For a lot of different people, regardless of how studious you are, this is a very difficult topic because of the whole academic environment. Since we are told when we are at university, we should be studying constantly and I think for every one hour of university teaching, you're meant to do five hours of independent learning.

I'm still can't (or refuse to) remember how many times I got told that during my first year.

However, the point is during our university life, we are told we are meant to do a lot of studying and revising and preparing for exams.

As a result, this leads to us to believe that we cannot afford to take any time off or do anything fun otherwise we risk our chances at a very good grade.

The reality?

To be honest, if you work really hard, at all hours of the day and you never have time for yourself. Then something very simple will happen to you. You burn out, become overwhelmed and you will just not want to study (or you at least won't retain the information you're trying to absorb. But that's a different blog post altogether).

Meaning you will theoretically be doing all the

right things by studying hard, but you'll burn out and you will forget the information you learn. Leading to bad grades.

The solution?

You simply need to be kind to yourself during exam season and make sure you have a balance between studying and having time for yourself.

How Do You be Kind To Yourself?

In my experience, there are four main ways for you to be kind to yourself for exams.

The first is very easy. You don't push yourself to the extreme. Now everyone has very different levels of comfort when it comes to studying. Some people can revise for half an hour at a time with a ten minute break then go back to it. Other people can revise for hours at a time without a break.

Personally and this is sort of degree-informed, I should recommend you do have regular breaks and maybe stick with half an hour to an hour revision sessions. But you need to do what works for you.

Secondly, it's important to make sure you work hard, but not to the extreme. It's good for everyone to push themselves slightly but only if that push benefits them. For example, if you believe you can only effectively revise three topics a day. Maybe try to revise a fourth, that way you get to revise more in the long term.

However, if you do that and you realise that fourth topic wasn't done as effectively as the first three. And it made you feel really tired, then maybe stick to your three topics a day. You just need to experiment and see what works for you.

As a saying goes in clinical psychology: *you are the expert in you.* So only you know what works for you and your revision, but be willing to try other things.

Revision Comparison:

Thirdly, and I was extremely confused when I first heard people do this, please do not compare yourself to other people. Of course, I know people compare themselves to others for things like bodies (don't do that), relationships and more. But I didn't know some people compare others for the amount of revision they do.

Now that is just... silly, and I must stress to you, please do not do that. Not only will that lead to a decrease in revision and an increase in burnout over the long term, but it'll just make you feel miserable. Why put yourself through that?

Therefore, if you feel yourself compare the amount of revision you do to someone else. Just stop. Focus on your own revision, do your best and make time for relaxing and you should be fine.

Actively Plan Your Relaxation Time

Finally (and this is the most important point), you need to actively plan your relaxation time and make sure you actually do things away from your revision area some days. Like, go out with friends and family, go to different places, go to the beach. Just go somewhere where you can unwind, relax and re-energised so you can come back to the textbooks and be ready to absorb more information for your exams.

Personally, during exam season, I make sure I go out with friends and family and I go out before exam season to different places. This allows me to be energised and ready for the exam season. For example, if this was my exam season this year, it would be good that I'm going up to London for a few days for a major international conference. This would allow me to study hard for a few days before I went, relax during the conference and then return re-energised afterwards.

Therefore, I doubt anyone of you go to conferences, but there are other parts of my example that you can take. Like going out with friends and family members.

Also, if you need something relaxing for a few hours, [read a book](#), watch a film or do something else. Just make sure you do relax.

How To Find A Balance During Exam Season?

Bearing all of that in mind, you need to make sure you don't spend so much time relaxing that you don't get any studying done. It's a strange paradox. Leading someone (probably you or me) to ask the question of how do you find a balance?

And if you remember the last exam season post: *How Should University Students Prepare for Exam Season*, you should factor in relaxation time into your revision schedule. As well as this serves an extremely important for you. It makes sure the revision timetable is something that you stick to because instead of it being a tortuous, boring chore. It will be something you're more likely to enjoy because you know if you do X amount of studying, you get to do Y as a relaxation reward afterwards.

Overall, just try to strike a balance between studying and being kind to yourself. Maybe go for 50:50, 60:40 (studying: relaxing) or whatever helps you do the best you can possibly do.

Conclusion:

We've spoken about a lot of things in this blog post, but here are the highlights:

- Be kind to yourself to avoid burnout
- Factor in some relaxation time by going out and doing things you enjoy. These activities will help you feel re-energised.
- Strike a balance between enough study time so you get good grades, with enough relaxation time to avoid burnout.

I hope you learnt something!

HOW TO REMAIN CALM DURING A UNIVERSITY STUDENT?

It is very common to feel stressed out during an exam, students panic, convince themselves they'll fail and lots of negative things can happen during the exam. As well as this is what's missed a lot when people talk about exam stress, they talk about the stress before and after the exam. But never the exam itself. Therefore, in this chapter, I'll tell you how to remain calm during a university exam.

<u>Believe In Yourself</u>

A lot of exam stress comes from you not believing in yourself, you might believe you'll fail the exam, not achieve what you want and your degree might be devastated by the exam if you don't do well on it.

At first glance, this all sounds logical, it sounds normal to believe in these things.

However, you're forgetting a very important thing about exams. You are an amazing university student, you've studied hard for the exam, you've practised and you've made sure you are as prepared for this exam as possible.

You need to remember this.

You haven't been one of these students who's panicking because they didn't do any revision or practice for it. You're a student who has tried to make sure they'll do well in the exam.

So please, stop putting so much pressure on yourself and start believing in yourself. Because there's an extremely high chance you're going to do amazing. I remember times when I thought I wasn't going to do well in an exam to be surprised later on, that's happened lots of different times.

There's no reason it can't happen to you.

You've got this, you just need to believe it!

<u>The World Won't End</u>

Another major factor I've heard from other university students is they believe the world will end if they don't get a certain grade in the exam. Of course you want to do well during your exams but you might come across a question that triggers all your fears about doing well in the exam.

In all honesty, the world will not end if you don't get a certain grade. Life will continue and so will your degree, because I'll tell you now, it is extremely difficult to fail a university exam. Since a fail is 40%.

Therefore, I'm saying, yes do your hardest to get the best exam result you can. But don't stress out about it, your world will continue if you don't.

Also I should note from personal experience that external influence (parents, friends and more) can put pressure on you during an exam. Their expectations can pop up at the worse times, but they don't matter in an exam. This isn't their life, their exam, their degree.

Personally I would like to see some of my family members try and answer some of the questions I've had to do for my exams. They couldn't do them, I know that for sure.

All in all, when you're in an exam, no one else matters and your world will continue. Thus, just try your best and answer every single question.

<u>Do The Exam</u>

Building upon the last section, you just need to put away all of the critical voice and just do the exam. It's better you tried your hardest in the exam and get a bad mark, than not doing the exam because of fears and stress, and getting a bad mark.

In my opinion I would remember what I've said in this blog post, your world will continue, what other people think doesn't matter and believe in yourself. Then just carry on with the exam.

I know it's hard sometimes but you aren't doing the exam for other people, you aren't doing it so you can compare with your friends. You're doing it because you want to develop your knowledge and get a grade for your future career.

But even then, it is just an exam at the end of the day. It isn't going to hurt you and as long as you've tried your best. Then that's all you can do.

<u>Conclusion:</u>

Overall, I hope you found this blog post useful and you now have some things to bear in mind and remember when you're next in an exam. I know it's difficult but we do need to get through the critical voice and do the exam.

I hope you found it useful and I wish you all the best of luck on your next exam!

HOW TO DEAL WITH STRESS AND ANXIETY AWAITING UNIVERSITY EXAM MARKS?

After you've done your exams and revision, there comes a time for some people where they are stuck waiting for their marks and they hate it. It can lead to stress and anxiety and this really hurts their mental health.

Hopefully, after reading this next chapter I can spare you some or if not all of this emotional pain.

We all hate waiting for the marks, but some people have other side effects. I really hope this helps.

Enjoy!

<u>How To Deal With Stress and Anxiety When Waiting For Exam Marks?</u>

After recently going through this myself, I understand why some students get stressed and anxious whilst they wait for their university marks. Personally, I had to wait to find out if I was going on my placement year and the uncertainty of my next university year was awful.

In this post, I'll explain some tips and tricks to help you deal with this stress and anxiety. Mainly we'll be focusing on the mental health side of this topic because this is what can harm you over time.

Why Is Waiting for Exam Marks Stressful?

I wanted to add this section because I really want you to know that you aren't the only university student feeling like this. We all get nervous, anxious and stressed out about our exams.

After an entire year of hard work, hard deadlines and almost impossible lectures, we need to know we've done well.

We need to know we've been successful.

Sadly, there's a large time delay between our exams and us getting our results. This can't be helped but it's still stressful.

Enjoy The Time Delay

My first big tip to you is reframe how you see this time delay between the exams and results. Don't see this as a scary time until you know your fate for the next university year.

See it as an amazing reward and three months off university for you to enjoy. This links to the other blogs on the website about Relaxation and enjoying yourself.

Therefore, I suggest you make the most of this time by going out with friends and family, doing what you love and having fun. Because I know from experience it isn't long until you're back at university again!

Your Feelings Are Temporary

I borrowed this tip from a podcast I'll link to down below and this is important. Due to your feelings of stress and anxiety are temporary. You aren't going to feel them forever.

As a result, you can bear this in mind, allow yourself to feel what you're feeling but know these feelings will go away.

Other Stress Reduction Tips:

I could easily talk about stress reduction for ages but we need to talk about the marks themselves.

The University Marks

With this being the source of a person's anxiety and stress, it's important to talk about them.

First and foremost, there are just marks. They are your results on a standardised test that show your knowledge at a point in time. They aren't the end of the world and if you're reading a blog like this then chances are, you've tried your best. That's all anyone can ask of you.

Expectations of Marks and Getting What You need

Leading me onto another point, please don't set your expectations too high. For example one of my university friends, he's extremely smart and he rightfully sets his expectations high. But he was disappointed with a 75 before because he expected an 80 something.

At the end of the day, that result is still a very good first but he got disappointed because his expectations were off.

In terms of you, I want to say adjust your expectations accordingly to protect yourself from disappointment. For example, we know the standard is a 2:1 at university which is at least a 60. As well as with a 2:1 you can get into graduate programmes (hopefully), do years in industry and more.

Therefore, if you're stressing out that you need a first or a score of 70. Ask yourself why? Are you setting expectations higher than needed?

Of course, try to get a first (if you want) but it's okay if you only get a 60.

Conclusion:

Overall, the point of this blog post is to emphasise I know waiting for university marks is horrific. But you need to relax and focus on the free time you now have.

However, if your marks are concerning you then make sure you understand you only need to get what you need for your next stage of university.

I know this is a very difficult topic but I hope you found it useful.

Have a great day!

ONLINE EXAMS FOR UNIVERSITY STUDENTS

In case you do end up doing online exams, then I thought it might be helpful for you to understand how it feels, especially if you're experiencing this for the first time, so the focus of the next chapter is telling you my own experience of these types of exams. In an effort to relax and help you and hopefully reveal what they're actually like compared to all the myths.

Online Exams For University Students: A Student's Perspective

When I was asked to write this post, I was rather pleased actually. Since it isn't often I get to do a blog on purely my own experience, and I really want to stress to all of you university students that online exams aren't evil, more difficult than in-person exams nor something to be scared of. So by the end of this post, you should start feeling more confident about online exams and I'll share with you my own experience with them.

Of course everything in this post is just my own opinions and experiences, and things might be different for you. But this post is filled with great concepts and ideas that you can draw on.

What Did I Think of Online Exams Before I Took Them?

I won't lie to you.

When I first learnt that I was going to be doing my exams online for the foreseeable future in April 2020, I was concerned. I didn't know how they were going to work, if they would be fair and if I would do terrible at them.

I'm hardly the only person to feel like this, so if you're concerned about them. You aren't alone but you don't need to feel like this for a few different reasons. Some of which I'll discuss now.

If you're in your first year at university and you have online exams, in my experience you have it the easiest like I did. Since our first university exams are almost always multiple choice questions and we simply need to choose the right answer.

If these are your exams then you really don't have anything to worry about, because the online exam is identical to the real in-person exam. You simply click on the correct answer.

Personally, I was really glad to have my first year exams online, because they were easy to do and I managed to get them done very quickly. Of course, NEVER rush exams and always check over your answers, but the nice thing about online exams is once you've done them. You can go.

And considering I had a forensic psychology exam on my birthday, I didn't want to do an exam for any longer than I had to.

However, I'm sure some of you are wondering about "proper" exams for second and third year students.

How Did I feel About my Second Year Exams Being Online?

This is where the student perspective comes in, because I would never say this section in public or in front of lecturers.

Since I was extremely pleased with my second year exams being online, because I am not the best academic writer. Give me a nonfiction or fiction book, a short story or a blog post, and I can write that easily enough. But give me an essay to write and I flaunter massively.

Thanks to the great people at my placement, I don't think that will be as much of the case next year, but during my second year I was very bad at academic writing. I knew the information like the back of my hands, but according to the university professors, I couldn't phrase the information in an academic manner to their liking.

Now I made that clear because I want other people who struggle with academic writing to know that things can improve (If you try to improve).

Anyway, online exams are great for people like

me because of one very special reason.

That is the university knows people will cheat and some modules try to remedy the situation. It goes without saying but don't cheat in your exams, that will only hurt you in the long run. But most of my essay writing exams during my second year were changed from closed book to open book exams, meaning I could have textbooks and notes around me.

Now this is flat out ideal because my problem with university exams is each lecture can be broken down into tens of little subareas, each of which could be an essay question. Therefore, I find the idea of revising for essays to be extremely daunting and I have no idea how I will manage in my third year.

However, with online exams tending to be open book that solves that problem. Online exams in my experience allow you to have your textbooks and notes around you.

Personally I think that was a lifesaver during my second year, and this is what I mean when I say online exams aren't scary or evil things. If you understand how to approach them, they can actually be extremely positive things.

Still I need to add, always check your exams because some of them might still be closed book, and of course don't cheat. Cheating is never good and it will seriously harm you in the long term, and you really don't want to be kicked out of university for something as silly as cheating in an exam.

Conclusion:

Looking back at my online exam experience, I won't lie- it was great. It was great to have slightly different exams that positively affected me. I know lots of people do find academic writing difficult even if they know the information, since universities just expect you to know how to write academically.

But that's a different blog post.

So I want to finish up by saying that online exams… they aren't scary, concerning or something you need to get anxious about. Exams are important for sure, but online exams can be great things if you know how to approach them.

Never see anything at university as a chore or evil because that will only lead to you feeling sad, down and like university isn't fun. And you should never feel like that. So please, look at online exams as something interesting to experience and maybe even a slightly better alternative to the traditional in-person exams we all grew up doing.

THIRD YEAR SURVIVAL GUIDE

MY FAVOURITE MOMENTS

To wrap up this book, I thought it would be fun to mention some of my favourite moments from my Final Year, just so you can start to understand what you have to look forward to in your own, as well as it will help to end the book on a positive note. Something that I think is absolutely critical.

And I mention some deeply personal things in this chapter too.

<u>Making Friends</u>

This is something that the vast majority of people can relate too in their Final Year, because yes you will typically have made friends in your first and second year but in your final year you also get to mix with new people so you can bond over your project, hopefully become friends and then keep in contact in the future.

As I mentioned earlier in the book, this was extremely important to me this year. Not only because I am autistic so friendship is always difficult, hard and a little impossible at times. But the COVID-19 pandemic and my placement resulted in me being stuck at home for two or three years meaning that my ability to socialise, meet people and more was greatly impacted.

Therefore, the ability to meet new people, talk to them and just become friends with them has been wonderful this year, and I cannot thank them enough for all the laughs and more that we've given each other over the past year.

For example, me and the girl I was working with on the project, we had a lot of fun together. We laughed, cried and we both agreed that without the other we seriously couldn't have done this year at all.

Another great example of friendships was the two activity-based lab socials we did. Bouldering was a lot of fun with all of them, and everyone was impressed with my strengths and then kayaking was a hell of a lot of fun too, as was the picnic afterwards and going back to one of the university's bars after that.

That had to be one of the best afternoons of my Final year. I loved every minute of it and yeah, those friends, those people, those activities were great fun and they were amazing.

I will definitely keep in contact with them and I've said to them that we need to keep in contact, meet up and stay friends, so I really hope that that does happen.

Overall, when it comes to your Final year at

university, you can look forward to it because it is a great opportunity to meet people, forge new friendships and just have fun.

Finding Acceptance And Improving Mental Health

I wanted to move onto two slightly "darker" favourite moments before we wrap up with another two positive ones, because this is important to understand. As if you have been through this then it is great to know that you can overcome it and if you haven't (you are very lucky) then it comes to be aware of what other people can go through in life.

Therefore, as a young gay man, I come from a background, family and social groups that do not like gays at all. They believe all the myths about gays being evil, criminals and more and they have no problem having anti-gay conversations in front of me.

I spoke about different angles of this in June 2023 on The Psychology World Podcast, so if you want to understand the psychology behind LGBT+ and homophobia then definitely check it out.

Anyway, as you can imagine this does take its toll on a person over time. Leaving me with some very bad Negative Automatic Thoughts, like *everyone hates me, everyone will abandon me, I am nothing, no one cares about me* and more.

Not exactly the best mental health whenever one of those thoughts gets activated, and if you've done clinical psychology before you know how getting mental health support is impossible for two main reasons. I have bad mental health but not to clinically significant levels and I can still function and I don't have a mental health condition.

Also, it doesn't help that I still live in a homophobic family that because of the state of the economy and the UK housing market, it is impossible to move out for at least the next two years.

Anyway, my point about my final year is that because I met amazing friends, amazing people and I "secretly" took LGBT+ Outreach events as a student ambassador I got to talk and mix with people that I never would have been allowed to mix with otherwise.

We got to share experiences, talk about my own and just have fun together. We could just be ourselves whenever I was on these events.

Then when it came to my friends, they didn't judge me, they didn't hate me and they didn't care that I was gay. And it helped to remind me that not everyone else hates me.

Therefore, whilst my mental health will always be questionable whenever one of my Negative Automatic Thoughts get activated, I have to admit that my friends during my Final Year have resulted in me no longer believing that *everyone hates me* and *everyone will abandon me*.

That is a massive relief.

On the whole, my point here is that if you have been through trauma, hate and more. Then your Final Year can be a good place to recover, learn what the "real" world is like and you can be around people that respect and accept you for you and don't hate you. It is a valuable lesson, and I know I will still need professional help in the future (when I can afford private therapy) but it is helpful for now.

And that is all because of my Final Year at university, something I will always be grateful for.

Having Opportunities

Moving back onto positive things, something I was surprised at was how many opportunities there are at university. Of course, I only ever had my First year on campus, and because everyone is always adapting to university life we don't notice what other opportunities are around us.

Therefore, in my Final year, I got to work on other projects, got to have conversations about Masters and a possible PhD project that will probably not get funding, but if it does then my supervisor says he wants me on the project.

Also, there are other opportunities outside of psychology. For example, there were a lot of opportunities through the Outreach department, like the LGBT+ Mythbusters sessions that show LGBT+ students that they can go to university just like straight people, and there were other chances to mix and talk to other ambassadors.

That was surprising at first because I hadn't done in-person Outreach events for two years, so it was so nice to talk to different ambassadors in different years on different courses. It was nice to get out of the psychology niche at times.

Overall, in your final year, if you open your eyes and you want to explore, then you will probably find a lot of great opportunities at your university that are important, a lot of fun and will certainly make you smile. Which after all the stress you might experience during the Final year Project that can certainly be a godsend.

So please, have a look, have fun and make a positive difference at the same time.

<u>Having a Future</u>

For the final main benefit of this year, I'm not really sure this can be classed overall as negative or positive (positive though) but I loved my final year at university, because it actually gave me a future.

I spoke earlier in the book about my "Bad" grades in my first and second year and how I was stressed, annoyed and being hard on myself that I might never get a 2:1 that I needed for my masters. Something I seriously wanted more than anything.

Then there was all the self-doubt and concerns that I had with my mental health and more, but over time as I spoke to more people, developed more relationships and mixed with LGBT+ people. I learnt that everything was okay and there was one person that sort of had a great impact on me.

During one of these Outreach events I met a trans-man (so he was a female at birth) and he had had an awful experience with his parents (they were Eastern European so never the most gay friendly in the first place. *His words not mine*). And we were just talking, laughing about our own experiences, spoke about his boyfriend and we kept in contact after the experience.

We remained friends and he sort of helped me to realise something that I already knew and something I always say to people, but maybe I had stopped believing it myself. Yet whatever you go through, whether you're straight or gay, things will get better in the future. It will take years at times for things to improve but it will get better and then you can start to live the life that *you* want for yourself.

Therefore, when that happened in addition to my later excellent grades, I realised that I am looking forward to the future and that is actually what I want to end this book with.

I am looking forward to the future because I know I will get my Masters, work my hardest through that time and I will have fun along the way. I have some work experience and volunteering booked so I can hopefully continue to build up my work experience before I graduate so I can go into the psychology job market with a bit of experience under me.

And then I can get a job, earn enough money to get a mortgage and then move away for good.

Then I can explore what being gay means to me as well as what being an adult means. I know this isn't applicable for everyone, but after your final year you are free to do whatever you want.

You can do a Masters, get a job, get work

experience, do whatever helps you achieve your goals and aims and dreams.

I know I am not the same person as I was when I started my Final Year. That man was even more damaged than I am, he didn't have a lot of friends and he certainly didn't have hope for a future.

But now, I do.

My final year has given me so much to look forward to and now I know that my future can be whatever I plan it to be. And I am one step closer to getting a high paid psychology job (yes I know I am still years away but still) and then I can just go out into the world.

And finally be free to love whoever I want, make friends with whoever I want and just enjoy life like so many others do.

I love my life, I really do, and I look forward to the future even more.

That is what your final year is all about. Learning, having fun and making friendships that will last a lifetime.

Enjoy.

MY FINAL YEAR PROJECT

Abstract

Transfer Effect has been proposed to explain how retrieval practice can improve learning, although there is no neuroevidence for this behavioural mechanism. This study proposes using theta brain oscillation (4-8 Hz) can quantify effort allowing the longer-term impacts of Retrieval-based learning to be explained using neuroevidence for the first time. Furthermore, this study suggests Long-Term Potentiation and Neural Efficiency Hypothesis can explain why Transfer Effect occurs from a neuroevidence standpoint. This study used a mixed factorial design (N=50) where participants took part in a learning task extended over several sessions where they continuously retrieved target materials. Then participants where assessed on their long-term retention of this material. The study demonstrated despite participants learning novel stimuli in each session, the task led to an increase in performance across the sessions, supporting the presence of Transfer Effect. Lastly, the study showed Frontal Midline Theta was associated with effort as it decreased from the first to last learning session, showing the participants found the task easier over time. Suggesting Frontal Midline Theta is a useful quantifier of effort and does provide neuroevidence for Transfer Effect. Then implications on the Retrieval-Based learning and Transfer Effect literature are discussed, highlighting how biological processes underpin this behavioural process, and how this links to meta-learning protocols used by the participant.

Investigating Oscillatory Activity Associated Transfer Learning

Learning is critical in everyday life from learning how to ride a bike to how to revise effectively for exams to how to drive a car, learning is everywhere, and learning requires several cognitive skills including memory retrieval as retrieval enhances learning (Roediger & Karpicke, 2006), leading to the development of retrieval-based learning (RBL) tasks, were learners' re-access newly learnt stimuli by undergoing tests. Typically, participants in an RBL task have an initial learning phase, where learners are tested on said stimuli, next is a testing phase, where the learners are tested on this material. RBL tasks utilise various combinations of these study-test blocks. Such as, STST, STTT, etc (Pyke et al., 2021). In control conditions, learners will not be tested on learnt material and all learners complete a final assessment to measure their overall learning, with these assessments taking place minutes (Smith et al., 2013) or months (Carpenter et al., 2009) after the previous phases. RBL tasks are beneficial for various populations, including patients (Friedman et al., 2017), children (Lipowski et al., 2014) and older adults (Coane, 2013) and RBL reliably shows increased long-term retention of learnt stimuli compared to study-only conditions (Agarwal et al., 2008; Fazio & Marsh, 2019; Karpicke & Grimaldi, 2012; Roediger & Butler, 2011).

The concept of learning via retrieval started in the early 20th century (Abbott, 1909; Gates, 1917, Spitzer, 1939) and Bjork's (1994) Desirable Difficulties Framework fits with RBL as it proposes an effective way to improve long-term retention of learnt stimuli is to introduce a desirable amount of difficulty (effort) whilst learning. Several models have been put forward to explain the efficacy of RBL. For example, Transfer Appropriate Processing (TAP) or Transfer Effect is the proactive use of prior learning in a novel context (Pan & Rickard, 2018) with a novel context potentially referring to any situation that is somehow different to the content the learning originally took place in (McDaniel, 2007). For example, a different test type, topic or goal (Barnett & Ceci, 2002). This links to effort because the TAP proposes a process of spreading activation occurs during the search for answers on a test (Anderson, 1996; Collins & Loftus, 1975; Raaijmakers & Shiffrin, 1981), creating multiple retrieval cues to aid later recall. This results in the testing effect (Pan & Rickard, 2018) and Pan and Rickard (2018) believed Transfer Effects could result from the same mechanism, because semantically-related information similar to previously learnt stimuli needs to be recalled on a transfer test. Therefore, the process of spreading activation that presumably occurs during the initial testing increases the likelihood this learnt information will be recallable as well (Carpenter, 2011; Chan, 2009; Chan, McDermott, & Roediger, 2006; Cranney, Ahn, McKinnon, Morris, & Watts,

2009) suggesting participants implicitly employ techniques to carry out learning resulting in effort likely being reduced. Overall, Pan and Rickard (2018) concluded test-enhanced learning could yield transfer performance substantially better than non-testing re-exposure conditions. This supports this paper's examination as our RBL task will help to provide further evidence for the efficacy of test-enhanced learning and Transfer Effects.

Furthermore, there are several biological processes that could be responsible for Transfer Effects. For example, Long-term Potentiation (LTP) is the strengthening of synapses based on recent neural activation producing a long-lasting increase in information transmission between two neurons (Cooke and Bliss, 2006). LTP underpins neuroplasticity (Bliss and Collingridge, 1993), this relates to Transfer Effect because memories are believed to be encoded according to synaptic strength. Hence, LTP is a major mechanism behind learning and memory (Bliss and Collingridge, 1993; Cooke and Bliss, 2006) possibly aiding in the process of spreading activation and creating retrieval cues for later recall as TAP proposes. Also, the Neural Efficiency Hypothesis proposes during a cognitive task, people with higher brain activation compared to low activation will be more successful at the task (Dunst et al., 2014) suggesting performance differences are caused by differences in the efficacy of a person's neural processing (Neubauer and Fink, 2009). Hence, this supports Transfer Effect because it would explain neurologically why some participants are better at a task compared to others, and presumably not as able to apply learning across similar contexts when learning new stimuli. Therefore, this paper will investigate transfer effect using Electroencephalogram (EEG) to provide supporting evidence for the neural basis of transfer effects, something not done until now.

In addition, EEG measures neuron electrical activity in the brain (Wu et al., 2016) and depending on the type of memory being retrieved different brain areas require different neural oscillations for successful encoding (Khader et al., 2010). For instance, stronger alpha activity was found in occipital-to-parietal scalp sites for subsequently remembered stimuli, and stronger theta power was found for subsequently remembered stimuli over parietal-to-central electrodes. Hence this suggests alpha and theta oscillations modulate successful LTM encoding (Khader et al., 2010) and theta activity is involved in working memory maintenance (Hsieh et al., 2014) with frontal theta oscillations playing a causal role in prioritizing WM representations (Riddle et al., 2020). Also, Nguyen et al. (2018) demonstrates how EEG can be used to quantify 'effort' in empirical investigations allowing this paper to empirically measure the effects of RBL on a participant's neuroactivity.

Furthermore, neural brain activity has a multitude of effects on WM which is involved in learning (Reber and Kotovsky, 1997; Schuler et al., 2011). For instance, frontal midline theta is critical for cognitive controls in and acts functionally different depending on task demands (Eschmann et al., 2018), and alpha brainwaves increase significantly during retrieval compared to demand and attentional tasks, and increasing alpha synchronisation with memory retrieval increases good memory performance (Klimesch et al., 1993). Suggesting a decrease in alpha synchronisation always leads to a decrease in memory performance, and supporting the role of brain oscillatory activity in memory. Further, when theta power increases during the memory encoding of words, more words are remembered later on and alpha power decreases during encoding yet did not always show significant differences in the alpha band between words remembered and not remembered (Klimesch and Doppelmayr, 1996). These human results are supported by animal studies as well, since Jutras and Buffalo (2014) demonstrated changes in medial temporal lobe activity across multiple frequency bands associated with stimulus novelty, familiarity, memory reactivation, temporal resolution, associative learning, and memory encoding provided evidence that neural oscillations could influence interactions between neurons during learning to encourage the formation of functional networks ready for later activation for consolidation or retrieval. Hence lending supporting evidence to how transfer effects could work in the brain.

Therefore, whilst no paper until now has provided neuro-evidence for Transfer Effect, this paper aims to see how the brain reflects the amount of effort university students put into learning because of transfer effect techniques by measuring differences in EEG activity in Session 1 and Session 5. This paper hypotheses theta activity will decrease in participants from Session 1 to Session 5. Also this paper seeks to examine performance improvement over time, predicting despite participants learning novel stimuli in each training session, they will improve between Session 1 to Session 5, indicating transfer effects.

Methods

Participants

G*Power 3.1.9.7 was used to run a priori power analysis and as a result 50 participants were recruited using volunteer sampling through the Research Participation Scheme at the University of Kent with an age range of 19-32 years old (M= 20) and 43 were female. Exclusion criterion for the study included any previous knowledge of any logographic language, being left-handed, having learning difficulties, like dyslexia and not being 17-32 years old. Yet participant nationality and ethnicity demographics were not collected. All participants received payment for their participation. The payment was £10 for RPS participants.

Design

Our quasi-experimental study used a mixed factorial design, with one ratio and two categorical independent variables (IVs), these were: Performance, Session, and Block. The dependent variables (DVs) for the study were Successful Retrievals, Response Latency, Untimed Cued-Recall Score, and Theta Power. For operationalisations of the variables, see Statistical Analyses, with a controlled variable being the day on which each session occurred.

Materials

Task Equipment

Our RBL-variation task required the use of a computer with two monitors, one for the participant to see the material on, and another for the experimenter to mark the responses correct/incorrect. The participants were never able to see the experimenter's screen. The participant used a keyboard to indicate their response, whilst the experimenter marked this using a mouse. During free recall testing, participants were recorded using the experimenter's mobile phone; this was labelled using an anonymous code and the recordings were deleted after the scores had been tallied. The software used to run the task was MATLAB Version 2021b (MathWorks, 2021).

EEG Equipment

EEG was set up with a WaveGuard 10/10 layout EEG cap consisting of 32 Ag/AgCl electrode channels. A standard measuring tape was used to measure the circumference of participants head for their cap size. The conductive gel was inserted into the electrodes using a syringe, the tip of which was replaced for each new participant. Also, a Wilcoxon signed rank test was used to analyse this data because the data was not normally distributed.

Stimuli

The stimuli used included 48 Japanese symbols, all of which were collected from https://www.learn-japanese-adventure.com/japanese-words.html. A previous study, that developed the current stimuli bank, examined the features and difficulties of these items (Pyke, Lunau, & Javadi, submitted for publication).

Procedure

General Procedure

The study consisted of 7 sessions. In the initial session, before completing any training, participants were asked to complete a baseline assessment to ensure that they had no prior knowledge of the symbols used in the study. During the first 5 training sessions, 8 novel symbol-word pairs were learnt by the participants, and EEG was administered in sessions 1 and 5 only. The first 5 training sessions were consecutive to each other. The sixth training session took place 3 days after session 5, where participants were exposed to all the symbols they had learnt in the previous sessions. This was done to control for primacy and recency effects, based on findings from Pyke et al. (2020). Aside from this, session 6 followed the same general procedure as the previous five. The testing session took place 4 days after session 6. Whilst participants knew the aim of the study, they were told not to rehearse stimuli outside of the sessions.

Task Procedure

The RBL task was completed on a computer and actively involved another person (the experimenter). The Japanese symbol-English word pairs were presented in the form of cued-recall, the participant was shown a symbol and asked to recall the corresponding English word. If participants did not remember or know the English word, they were asked to say 'Go'. This was marked as 'incorrect', and the next symbol was presented. If the participant failed to respond within a few seconds, they were prompted by the experimenter to say 'Go' and continue onto the next symbol. This was recorded as an incorrect response as well. Along with every response, the participant was asked to click 'J' on their keyboard, which allowed the experimenter to mark their accuracy by a mouse-button click. Once the experimenter had marked the response, on-screen feedback was given to the participant. If they responded with the incorrect word, or said 'go', they were required to repeat the correct answer out loud. After the participant had correctly answered a symbol-word pair three consecutive times, the experimenter no longer needed to indicate accuracy, because it was assumed to be correct, and no further feedback was provided. This gave control of pace to the participant, allowing them to cycle through the material at a faster speed. If an incorrect answer was given at any point during this stage, the experimenter would interrupt the participant with the correct answer.

Final Test

The testing session consisted of three phases testing different aspects of participants' memory performance: timed free recall, untimed cued recall, and timed cued recall. The "testing pack" was specific to each participant. In the timed free recall phase, participants were given 1min to recall the English names for the symbols they had learnt during the six training sessions. In the untimed cued-recall phase, all 40 symbols were presented in random order and participants were asked to recall the corresponding English word without any time pressure. The timed cued-recall phase consisted of two 1-min blocks in which symbols were presented randomly. In all cued-recall phases, symbols were shown in the same manner as in the training sessions, except feedback was never provided. Incorrect and correct answers during all three cued-recall phases were marked by the researcher using a list generated prior.

Results

Behavioural Findings

We conducted a 5 x 10 (Session x Block) Repeated Measurement ANOVA examining the interaction between Session and Block on successful retrieval. The main effects of Block were significant but this violated Mauchly's test ($p < .01$), this was corrected with Greenhouse-Geisser correction. $F(1.49, 83.60)=588.57$, $MSE=46985.27$, $p <.001$. The main effects of Session, $F(4, 224)=71.81$, $MSE=32127.71$, $p <.001$, and the main effects of Session x Block violated Mauchly's test ($p < .01$), this was corrected with Greenhouse-Geisser correction. $F(9.43, 527.91)= 21.91$, $MSE= 30.22$, $p < .01$, demonstrating Session and Block does have a significant effect on a participant's successful retrieval. Further confirmed by the significance of all pairwise comparisons ($p < .01$).

Figure 1a- Mean Correct Responses Between Session 1-5

Figure 1a shows the results of T-tests finding participants had a significantly higher mean correct responses in Session 5 than Session 1 revealing $t(56)= 13.34$, $p <.001$. The effect size was large with a Cohen's d of 0.59.

Figure 1b- Mean Correct Response Between Session 1 Block 1 and Session 5 Block 1

Figure 1b further supports the ANOVA findings by showing the results of T-tests finding participants had a significantly higher mean correct responses in Session 5 Block 1 than Session 1 Block 1 revealing $t(55)= 14.36$, $p <.001$. The effect size was large with a Cohen's d of 1.92.

Figure 1c- *Mean Correct Response Between Session 1 Block 10 and Session 5 Block 10*

Figure 1c shows the results of T-tests finding participants had a significantly higher mean correct responses in Session 5 Block 10 than Session 1 Block 10 revealing t(55)= 10.15, p <.001. The effect size was large with a Cohen's d of 1.35.

Figure 2- Correlation Between Mean Correct Responses And Final Cued Recall Scores

Figure 2 shows the correlation between a participant's mean number of correct answers in Session and Block and their Final Cued Recall scores, indicating successful retrieval. There was a strong positive correlation between the two variables, r(49)= .584, p= (0.01) suggesting how well a participant does in Session and Block effects their Final Cued Recall scores.

Figure 3- Mean Correct Responses Between Block 1-10

Figure 3 shows the mean correct responses in each Block with error bars for the standard deviations of responses, showing participants got more correct responses as they were exposed to the Stimuli more as the Blocks progressed since the mean for Block 1 was 81.08 and Block 10 was 253.34.

Note. Based on normal means and standard deviations. Bars correspond to 95% confidence intervals.

Figure 4- Mean Correct Responses Cross Sessions 1-5

Figure 4 supports Figure 3 by showing the standard deviations for mean correct responses per Session, demonstrating like Figure 3 as participants continue the task over the Sessions, they get more correct responses. The mean for Session 1 was 188 and the Session 5 was 369.18.

Note. Based on estimated marginal means. Bars correspond to 95% confidence intervals.

We conducted a 5 x 10 (Session Response Time x Block Response Time) Repeated Measurement ANOVA examining the interaction between Session Response Time and Block Response Time on Response Latency. Session Response Time, Block Response Time and the interaction between the two variables violated Mauchly's test ($p < .01$), this was corrected with Greenhouse-Geisser correction. The main effects of Block Response Time were significant, $F(2.34, 130.88)=33.64$, MSE=31.63, $p <.01$. The main effects of Session Response Time, $F(3.12, 177.25)=71.44$, MSE=48.79, $p <.01$, and the main effects of Session Response Time x Block Response Time were $F(7.63, 427.45)= 2.08$, MSE= 0.44, $p < .04$, demonstrating Session Response Time and Block Response Time does have a significant effect on a participant's Response Latency. Both of these variables violated Mauchly's test ($p < .01$) so Greenhouse-Geisser corrections were needed. Further confirmed by the significance of all pairwise comparisons ($p < .01$).

Figure 5- Mean Response Times Between Session 1-5

Figure 5 shows the mean response times for participants between Session 1 and 5 showing participants get faster as Session progresses. The mean for Session 1 was 1.77 seconds and the mean for Session 5 was 1.19 seconds.

Electrophysiological Findings

Analysis of the averaged EEG data showed a

decrease in the frequency bands 4-8Hz suggesting frontal midline theta (Rutishauser et al., 2010), from the first to fifth training session as showed in Figure 6. The Wilcoxon signed-rank test demonstrated this difference was statistically significant ($Z=2.646$, $p = 0.008$). These statistics are the average activity over the region of interest (frequency = [3, 8], and time = [400, 850]. Although not all electrodes demonstrated activity.

Figure 6- *Neuroelectric Comparisons Between Sessions One and Five*

Note. Figure 6 shows the activity and differences in both sessions with the dashed rectangle showing the region of analysis.

Discussion

The current study set out to investigate Transfer Effects in RBL predicting participants would increase across a time period because of Transfer Effects. Further, this study examined whether frontal-midline theta, measured as a function of effort, decreases between Session 1 and Session 5 predicting effort would decrease.

This supported our hypothesis by demonstrating despite participants learning new stimuli each session, there is a statistically significant improvement between Session 1 and Session 5 (see Figure 1). This was further supported by our post-hoc tests being significant and Figure 3 and 4, because these Figures show further improvement to participants' scores across Sessions and Block. Hence, as this paper set out to investigate, our results show participants do improve between Session 1 and

Session 5 despite learning novel stimuli indicating Transfer Effects. Further, this hypothesis is supported by the statistically significant interaction between Session Response Time and Block Response on Response Latency and the supporting significant post-hoc tests. Due to our results and Figures 2 and 5 demonstrate over the 5 Sessions, participants get quicker and more accurate at responding correctly potentially showing the process of spreading activation occurring during a participant's search for answers on the RBL Task creating a multitude of retrieval cues to aid later recall, similar to the proposal and findings of Anderson (1996), Collins and Loftus (1975) and Raaijmakers and Shiffrin (1981) indicating Transfer Effects. Also, learning rate changes across Session indicating meta-learning (Transfer Effect).

Moreover, our results support previous literature about the Transfer and Testing Effect because as Pan and Rickard (2018) proposed participants are using their prior learning in the new context of each new session conducting the same task. This is what McDaniel (2007) found was needed for the Transfer Effect to occur. Also, this is similar to the findings of Pan and Rickard (2018) as they believed semantically-related information is what participants need to have actual recall later on, linking to the Testing Effect and Figure 2 as it shows the more correct responses a participant has in Session the more correct responses they give in Final Cued Recall tests. Moreover, our results in Figure 2 and 6 demonstrates the process of spreading activation that occurs in initial testing (Session) increases the likelihood of this learnt stimuli being called later on, similar to several other studies (Carpenter, 2011;

Chan, 2009; Chan et al., 2006; Cranney et al., 2009). Overall, theoretically our results provide additional supporting evidence for Transfer and Testing Effect and how these psychological principles impact memory retrieval during RBL tasks.

Further, this study did support our second hypothesis because this study find did a significant decrease in frontal midline theta (Fmθ) between T1 and T5 suggesting Fmθ modulates effort in RBL. This matches previous literature because this study found a decrease in Fmθ which lead to successful LTM encoding. These findings are similar to Khader et al. (2010) and our findings suggest EEG data can be used to investigate effort as Nguyen et al. (2018) proposed. However, our findings do not support other studies. For instance, Gevins et al. (1997) found an increase in both Alpha power and Fmθ after task practice where this study only found an increase in Fmθ. Therefore, our results are conflicting to this study. This could be because Gevins did not use a RBL paradigm in the study or task type, but this still demonstrates our results add to the body of literature supporting Fmθ modulates effort in learning and additional literature suggests Fmθ is highly related to cognitively demanding tasks and/or tasks requiring high mental concentration (Doppelmayr et al., 2008; Ishii et al., 2014).

Moreover, our finding of a decrease in Fmθ suggests whilst participants maximise their correct response scores, the participants apply meta-learning (Transfer Effects) protocols to minimise the cortical resources required for the task. This neurological data supports previous behavioural studies demonstrating the effectiveness of RBL tasks in aiding participant learning because our task enabled participants to complete the task more effectively by practising and this resulted in reducing the time and effort needed for successful retrievals. Therefore, whilst the theoretical implications are mixed because our results fit with some, but not all, literature. This paper further supports the argument of it is Fmθ, not alpha power modulating effort in RBL.

Our research findings have a plethora of practical implications. Since our research findings add to the validity and wider literature support for RBL interventions, this can be used to support RBL in education contexts, for example. RBL has a history of use in educational settings covering a range of settings. Sanders et al. (2019) demonstrated how RBL tasks can effectively teach medical students human anatomy better than students passively exposed to learnt material with the authors noting how RBL tasks can be applied to any educational setting. This has additional research support from other medical school studies, like Sya'ban et al. (2021) and different sectors within education from general education (Buchin and Mulligan, 2023) and special education settings (Gordon, 2020). Therefore, these findings show this paper's results could have implications throughout the education sector from the lower years in primary and secondary school all the way up to university-level students. RBL has the empirical backing in the literature to help all these students improve the amount of learnt material later recalled.

Furthermore, RBL tasks have several implications within clinical psychology since RBL is commonly used in word-learning contexts for children with learning disabilities. For instance, the review into RBL by Gordon (2020) found modern empirical evidence shows RBL can enhance word learning for children with learning disorders with there being guidance for clinicians on how to effectively apply RBL for word learning. Gordan (2020)'s findings are important for our results since this study used a word-learning task to teach students Japanese symbols, suggesting our results have direct implications for children with language disorders. This is further supported by additional studies, like Haebig et al. (2019), Leonard et al. (2019), Leonard et al. (2020) and Leonard and Deevy (2020). All finding RBL tasks help both typically-developing children and those with a language disorder learn novel word stimuli and experience long-term retention. Overall, a multitude of studies supports how our results can be used to implement real-world interventions to help children affected by developmental language disorders enhance their word learning, and given how language skills are highly predictable of a child's ability to read and success at school (Dickinson & Tabors, 2001; McCardle et al., 2001; Snow, Burns & Griffin, 2005; Snow et al., 1999; Stanovich et al., 1986; Storch & Whitehurst, 2001; Walker, Greenwood, Hart & Carta, 1994), this is an important problem needing an intervention. RBL tasks could be the intervention as showed in our results and those of other studies.

Our study had several limitations that need to be addressed in future research. Control groups are needed so researchers know if an intervention is working and these effects can be separated from the effects of other interventions (Pithon, 2013). Similar to how Randomised Controlled Trials (RCT) in clinical psychology research allow researchers to benefit from RCT being the most robust and empirical method for establishing whether a cause-and-effect relationships exists (Bhide et al., 2018). Although, our study did not use a control group so whilst our findings demonstrate our RBL task is helpful in participant learning and successful retrieval, this study cannot separate these effects from other interventions because this study cannot say if the successful retrieval was a result of our task or them doing a learning intervention regardless of the type used. Therefore, future research must use control groups to ensure the study's results are from the RBL intervention and not other variables.

Secondly, whilst our study found a decrease in $Fm\theta$ was related to learning and more success retrievals later on, this study did not investigate neuroelectric activity during the testing phase and since this study did not use a control group this study could not investigate cognitive effort in differentially difficult tasks. This would have given us more data to support our conclusions with and it would have made our study fit with additional literature. For example, Berry and Thompson (1978) found rabbits who showed higher theta activity learnt faster than rabbits with higher brain frequencies. Also, Mussel et al. (2016) found theta power reflects cognitive effort on tasks differing in difficulty and this is predictive of performance on these tasks. Together these studies demonstrate neuroelectric activity can be used to investigate motivational and effort mechanisms underpinning active learning tasks. Therefore, whilst our study did not look at these concepts, future research should investigate differences in neuroelectric differences between experimental and control groups to see whether such oscillatory differences can predict differences in performance to further add to the RBL literature.

Finally, whilst our study made used of a 1-week post-test element allowing us to understand the long-term impacts of our RBL intervention on participant performance, future research should make use of longer post-intervention periods to further understand the long-term effects of RBL. Since currently, this study can only say with empirical evidence, RBL is effective for one week following the intervention. Anything later this guessing. Also, this is a larger criticism of the RBL literature because a plethora of studies only use one-week post-intervention posts, like Agarwal et al. (2008), Karpicke and Grimaldi (2012) and Roediger and Butler (2011). Therefore, this limitation needs to be addressed in the literature because currently the longer term effects of RBL are unknown. Also, it is arguable the work of Sheffield and Hudson (2006), Memon et al. (1997) and Hudson (1990) nullifies this limitation because research shows improved retrieval of novel events and improved memory 8- and 12-weeks after learning. Yet RBL tasks were not used making the results difficult to compare and the research sample was 18-months old infants, pre-schoolers and elementary pupils, not adults. Hence, this limitation remains. Overall, future research should use different experimental groups with different post-intervention time periods, allowing researchers to learn if there is a limit or optimal gap between training and testing.

In conclusion, this study provides evidence that a RBL task is useful in learning and this study explores several behavioural and neurological mechanisms for this efficacy. Mainly meta-learning or Transfer Effect were responsible, because this effect promotes successful retrieval by applying learning across similar contexts requiring less effort to learn. This is consistent with our results and Transfer Effect is widely supported in the literature as an underlying principle of learning (Pan & Rickard, 2018). These findings have valuable implications for RBL theories, like Transfer Appropriate Processing theory and Long-term Potentiation, because this is the first time neuroevidence on Transfer Effects has been conducted, directing future research towards using control groups, longitudinal methodology and investigating neural oscillations during the testing phase. Also, our results can be practically applied in clinical and educational settings where using active learning procedures to boost learning and performance is on the rise (Wirth & Perkins, 2008).

https://www.subscribepage.com/psychologyboxset

CHECK OUT THE PSYCHOLOGY WORLD PODCAST FOR MORE PSYCHOLOGY INFORMATION! AVAILABLE ON ALL MAJOR PODCAST APPS.

About the author:

Connor Whiteley is the author of over 60 books in the sci-fi fantasy, nonfiction psychology and books for writer's genre and he is a Human Branding Speaker and Consultant.

He is a passionate warhammer 40,000 reader, psychology student and author.

Who narrates his own audiobooks and he hosts The Psychology World Podcast.

All whilst studying Psychology at the University of Kent, England.

Also, he was a former Explorer Scout where he gave a speech to the Maltese President in August 2018 and he attended Prince Charles' 70th Birthday Party at Buckingham Palace in May 2018.

Plus, he is a self-confessed coffee lover!

Other books by Connor Whiteley:
All books in 'An Introductory Series':
Careers In Psychology
Psychology of Suicide
Dementia Psychology
Clinical Psychology Reflections Volume 4
Forensic Psychology of Terrorism And Hostage-Taking
Forensic Psychology of False Allegations
Year In Psychology
CBT For Anxiety
CBT For Depression
Applied Psychology
BIOLOGICAL PSYCHOLOGY 3RD EDITION
COGNITIVE PSYCHOLOGY THIRD EDITION
SOCIAL PSYCHOLOGY- 3RD EDITION
ABNORMAL PSYCHOLOGY 3RD EDITION
PSYCHOLOGY OF RELATIONSHIPS- 3RD EDITION
DEVELOPMENTAL PSYCHOLOGY 3RD EDITION
HEALTH PSYCHOLOGY
RESEARCH IN PSYCHOLOGY
A GUIDE TO MENTAL HEALTH AND

TREATMENT AROUND THE WORLD-
A GLOBAL LOOK AT DEPRESSION
FORENSIC PSYCHOLOGY
THE FORENSIC PSYCHOLOGY OF
THEFT, BURGLARY AND OTHER
CRIMES AGAINST PROPERTY
CRIMINAL PROFILING: A FORENSIC
PSYCHOLOGY GUIDE TO FBI
PROFILING AND GEOGRAPHICAL
AND STATISTICAL PROFILING.
CLINICAL PSYCHOLOGY
FORMULATION IN PSYCHOTHERAPY
PERSONALITY PSYCHOLOGY AND
INDIVIDUAL DIFFERENCES
CLINICAL PSYCHOLOGY
REFLECTIONS VOLUME 1
CLINICAL PSYCHOLOGY
REFLECTIONS VOLUME 2
Clinical Psychology Reflections Volume 3
CULT PSYCHOLOGY
Police Psychology

A Psychology Student's Guide To University
How Does University Work?
A Student's Guide To University And Learning
University Mental Health and Mindset

<u>Bettie English Private Eye Series</u>
A Very Private Woman
The Russian Case
A Very Urgent Matter
A Case Most Personal
Trains, Scots and Private Eyes
The Federation Protects
Cops, Robbers and Private Eyes
Just Ask Bettie English
An Inheritance To Die For
The Death of Graham Adams
Bearing Witness
The Twelve
The Wrong Body
The Assassination Of Bettie English

<u>Lord of War Origin Trilogy:</u>
Not Scared Of The Dark
Madness
Burn Them All

<u>The Fireheart Fantasy Series</u>
Heart of Fire
Heart of Lies
Heart of Prophecy
Heart of Bones
Heart of Fate

<u>City of Assassins (Urban Fantasy)</u>
City of Death
City of Marytrs
City of Pleasure
City of Power

<u>Agents of The Emperor</u>
Return of The Ancient Ones
Vigilance
Angels of Fire
Kingmaker
The Eight
The Lost Generation
Hunt
Emperor's Council
Speaker of Treachery
Birth Of The Empire
Terraforma

<u>The Rising Augusta Fantasy Adventure Series</u>
Rise To Power
Rising Walls
Rising Force
Rising Realm
<u>Lord Of War Trilogy (Agents of The Emperor)</u>

THIRD YEAR SURVIVAL GUIDE

Not Scared Of The Dark
Madness
Burn It All Down

<u>Gay Romance Novellas</u>
Breaking, Nursing, Repairing A Broken Heart
Jacob And Daniel
Fallen For A Lie
Spying And Weddings

<u>Miscellaneous:</u>
RETURN
FREEDOM
SALVATION
Reflection of Mount Flame
The Masked One
The Great Deer
English Independence

OTHER SHORT STORIES BY CONNOR WHITELEY

<u>Mystery Short Story Collections</u>
Criminally Good Stories Volume 1: 20 Detective Mystery Short Stories
Criminally Good Stories Volume 2: 20 Private Investigator Short Stories
Criminally Good Stories Volume 3: 20 Crime Fiction Short Stories
Criminally Good Stories Volume 4: 20 Science Fiction and Fantasy Mystery Short Stories
Criminally Good Stories Volume 5: 20 Romantic Suspense Short Stories

<u>Mystery Short Stories:</u>
Protecting The Woman She Hated
Finding A Royal Friend
Our Woman In Paris
Corrupt Driving
A Prime Assassination
Jubilee Thief
Jubilee, Terror, Celebrations
Negative Jubilation
Ghostly Jubilation
Killing For Womenkind
A Snowy Death

THIRD YEAR SURVIVAL GUIDE

Miracle Of Death
A Spy In Rome
The 12:30 To St Pancreas
A Country In Trouble
A Smokey Way To Go
A Spicy Way To GO
A Marketing Way To Go
A Missing Way To Go
A Showering Way To Go
Poison In The Candy Cane
Kendra Detective Mystery Collection Volume 1
Kendra Detective Mystery Collection Volume 2
Mystery Short Story Collection Volume 1
Mystery Short Story Collection Volume 2
Criminal Performance
Candy Detectives
Key To Birth In The Past

<u>Science Fiction Short Stories:</u>
Their Brave New World
Gummy Bear Detective
The Candy Detective
What Candies Fear
The Blurred Image
Shattered Legions

The First Rememberer
Life of A Rememberer
System of Wonder
Lifesaver
Remarkable Way She Died
The Interrogation of Annabella Stormic
Blade of The Emperor
Arbiter's Truth
Computation of Battle
Old One's Wrath
Puppets and Masters
Ship of Plague
Interrogation
Edge of Failure

<u>Fantasy Short Stories:</u>
City of Snow
City of Light
City of Vengeance
Dragons, Goats and Kingdom
Smog The Pathetic Dragon
Don't Go In The Shed
The Tomato Saver
The Remarkable Way She Died
Dragon Coins
Dragon Tea
Dragon Rider

www.ingramcontent.com/pod-product-compliance
Lightning Source LLC
LaVergne TN
LVHW012105070526
838202LV00056B/5623